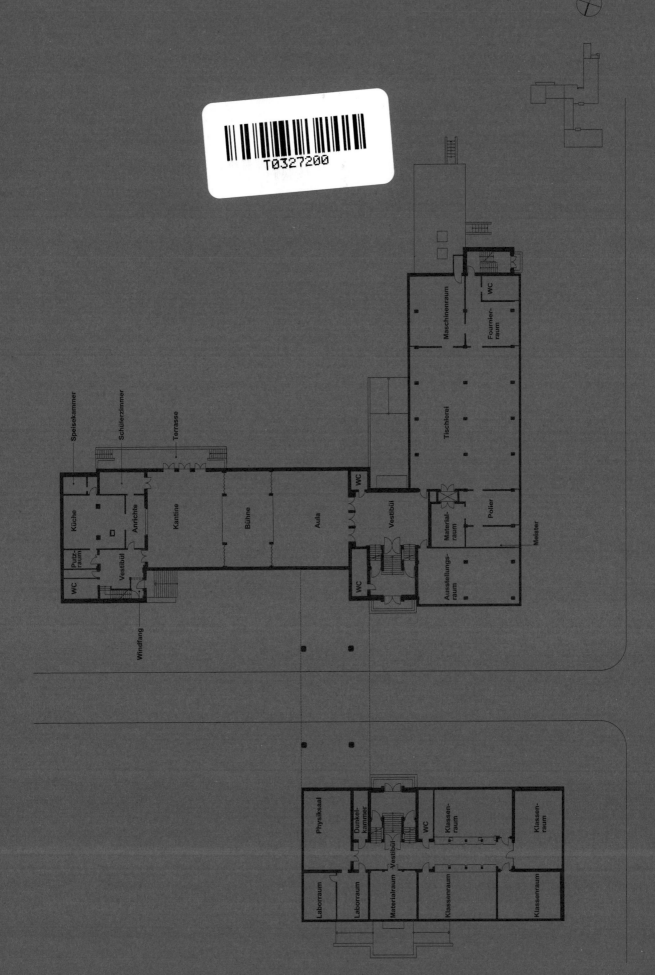

Grundriss Erdgeschoss ▪ Ground Plan Ground Floor, 1926

Labels on plan:

Speisekammer
Schülerzimmer
Terrasse
Küche
Anrichte
Kantine
Bühne
Aula
WC
Putz-raum
Vestibül
Windfang
WC
WC
Vestibül
Material-raum
Ausstellungs-raum
Polier
Meister
Maschinenraum
Fournier-raum
WC
Tischlerei

Physiksaal
Dunkel-kammer
Laborraum
Laborraum
Materialraum
Vestibül
WC
Klassenraum
Klassenraum
Klassenraum
Klassenraum

BAUHAUS DESSAU

Architecture Design Concept **Architektur Gestaltung Idee**

JOVIS

"IT IS A MISTAKE TO BELIEVE THAT THE MODERN MOVEMENT IS GUIDED SOLELY BY FUNCTIONALITY, AND NOT BY BEAUTY. THE OPPOSITE IS THE CASE".
Walter Gropius, 1928

„IRRTUM, WENN MAN GLAUBT, DASS DIE MODERNE BEWEGUNG SICH NUR VOM ZWECK LEITEN LASSE UND NICHT VON DER SCHÖNHEIT. DAS GEGENTEIL IST DER FALL."
Walter Gropius, 1928

BAUHAUS DESSAU

Architecture Design Concept **Architektur Gestaltung Idee**

Kirsten Baumann

JOVIS

HERAUSGEGEBEN VON DER STIFTUNG BAUHAUS DESSAU

Dedication Danksagung
I would especially like to thank for their help with this book
Mein Dank für die Unterstützung bei der Fertigstellung dieses
Buches gilt besonders
Torsten Blume, Martin Brück, Katrin Globke, Silvia Höll, Mo-
nika Markgraf, Doreen Ritzau, Margot Rumler, Sandra Scheer,
Katja Simon, Jutta Stein, Wolfgang Thöner und Petra Wel-
höner.

Content Inhalt

Prologue **Vorwort**

"The Bauhaus Building in Dessau is a seminal work of Modernism in Europe, embodying its avant-garde and radical revival of architectural and design concepts with a unique, interdisciplinary approach. In art historical terms, this is one of the most significant monuments of modern architecture". In 1996, the justification for its inclusion in the list of UNESCO World Heritage Sites gave two important reasons for our lasting fascination with the Bauhaus: its function as a pioneer of international Modernism, and its wide-ranging success as a school.

The Bauhaus was subject to both criticism and praise in equal measure. Today, it continues to be falsely interpreted as the supposed initiator of an artistic movement or "style". Gropius himself warned against this development in 1930: "the bauhaus was the first institution in the world that dared anchor this anti-academic ideal within a scholastic framework. (…) a 'bauhaus style', however, would be a throwback into academic stagnation, into that state of inactivity that threatens our existence, and which the Bauhaus was brought to life to combat. may the bauhaus be preserved from this kind of death!" (Walter Gropius, *Bauhausbauten Dessau*, 1930). The Bauhaus was both cornucopia and reservoir, and thrived on the creative impulses emerging from Europe and America. Thanks to Walter Gropius the right artists came together at the right time and place. They brought their avant-garde stance and radicalism to Weimar and Dessau, passing these on to their students, who in turn gave them to the wider world.

The Bauhaus Building as such is, above all, a "school of seeing" – a building with a didactic purpose. It encourages conscious engagement with its proportions, surfaces, forms and colour. You are invited to participate in a tour of the building, which today incorporates contemporary photographs documenting the building's condition after its comprehensive renovation, which ended in 2006. The reconstructed fixtures and fittings, such as furniture and lights, are to be seen. Short texts reveal facts about the former school's workshops and the lives of its teachers and students. Stay curious and open-minded throughout your tour of the building. Enjoy the spatial concepts as much as the fine details, scrutinize window mechanisms, and discover new perspectives.

The Bauhaus was a workshop and school building – a lively place. It was never a museum, and is still not one today. In 1994, the Federal Government of Germany, the State of Saxony-Anhalt and the municipality of Dessau established the Bauhaus Dessau Foundation as a scientific institution. This Foundation is based in the Bauhaus Building. Experience a lively Bauhaus, where research continues into important historical and topical issues and which, even after its structural restoration, has resisted becoming an open-air museum. The Bauhaus and its people would have shared your pleasure.

Omar Akbar
Director of the Bauhaus Dessau Foundation

„Das Dessauer Bauhausgebäude ist ein Schlüsselwerk der Moderne in Europa, verkörpert es doch deren avantgardistisches, auf radikale architektonische und gestalterische Erneuerung gerichtetes Konzept in einer einmaligen breitenwirksamen Konzentration. Dieses Gebäude muss kunstgeschichtlich als eines der bedeutendsten Denkmale des modernen Bauens gelten." Die Begründung für die Aufnahme in die UNESCO Welterbeliste nannte 1996 zwei wichtige Punkte für die bis heute anhaltende Faszination des Bauhauses: seine Funktion als Vorreiter einer internationalen Moderne und seine Breitenwirksamkeit als Schule.

Es ist mit ebenso viel Lob wie scharfer Kritik bedacht worden. Bis heute unterliegt das Bauhaus einer Fehlbewertung als vermeintlicher Initiator einer künstlerischen Bewegung oder eines Stils. Gropius selbst warnte schon 1930 davor: „als erstes institut in der welt hat das bauhaus es gewagt diese antiakademische geisteshaltung schulisch zu verankern. [...] ein ‚bauhausstil' aber wäre ein rückschlag in die akademische stagnation, in den lebensfeindlichen trägheitszustand, zu dessen bekämpfung das bauhaus einst ins leben gerufen wurde. vor diesem tod möge das bauhaus bewahrt bleiben!" (Walter Gropius, *Bauhausbauten Dessau*, 1930) Das Bauhaus war Füllhorn und Sammelbecken zugleich und lebte von künstlerischen Impulsen aus ganz Europa und den USA. Walter Gropius ist es zu verdanken, dass sich die richtigen Künstler zur richtigen Zeit am richtigen Ort versammelten. Sie brachten ihre avantgardistischen Positionen, ihre Radikalität mit nach Weimar und Dessau und gaben sie an ihre Schüler weiter, die sie in die ganze Welt trugen.

Das Bauhausgebäude selbst ist vor allem eine Schule des Sehens, ein Bau mit didaktischem Anspruch. Bewusst hinsehen soll man hier, auf Proportionen, Oberflächen, Formen und Farben achten. Sie sind eingeladen zu einem Rundgang durch das Gebäude, wie es sich heute präsentiert. Aktuelle Fotografien begleiten Sie dabei und dokumentieren den Zustand des Hauses nach dem Abschluss der umfassenden Sanierung im Jahr 2006. Die rekonstruierten Einrichtungsgegenstände wie Möbel und Leuchten sind zu sehen, kurze Texte geben Aufschluss über die damaligen Werkstätten der Schule sowie die Lebensverläufe ihrer Lehrer und Studierenden. Gehen Sie mit neugierigem und offenem Blick durch das Haus. Erfreuen Sie sich an Raumkonzepten ebenso wie an feinen Details, studieren Sie Fenstermechanismen und entdecken Sie ungewohnte Ansichten.

Das Bauhaus war ein Werkstatt- und Schulgebäude, ein lebendiger Ort – es war nie ein Museum und ist auch heute keines. 1994 wurde die Stiftung Bauhaus Dessau als wissenschaftliche Einrichtung durch die Bundesrepublik Deutschland, das Land Sachsen-Anhalt und die Stadt Dessau gegründet. Ihr Sitz ist das Bauhausgebäude. Erleben Sie ein lebendiges Bauhaus, in dem über wichtige historische und aktuelle Fragen geforscht wird und das auch nach der baulichen Wiederherstellung nicht zum Freilichtmuseum geworden ist. Die Bauhäusler hätten sich mit Ihnen gefreut.

Omar Akbar
Direktor der Stiftung Bauhaus Dessau

The Bauhaus in Weimar, Dessau and Berlin
Das Bauhaus in Weimar, Dessau und Berlin

Staatliches Bauhaus Weimar

Das Bauhaus verdankte seine Entstehung einer politischen Zeitenwende in Europa. Deutschland verlor den Ersten Weltkrieg, im November 1918 dankte Kaiser Wilhelm II. ab. Die Reichshauptstadt Berlin war noch von Unruhen geschüttelt, und so tagte die neue Nationalversammlung Anfang 1919 in Weimar. Im August trat die Weimarer Reichsverfassung in Kraft, die den Weg in ein neues, demokratisches Deutschland weisen sollte. Gerade im kulturellen Bereich herrschte Aufbruchstimmung, und vieles schien möglich.

„nach der brutalen unterbrechung der arbeit, die der krieg erzwang, ergab sich für jeden denkenden die notwendigkeit der umstellung. jeder sehnte sich von seinem gebiet aus, den unheilvollen zwiespalt zwischen wirklichkeit und geist zu überbrücken. sammelpunkt dieses willens wurde das bauhaus." (Walter Gropius, *Bauhausbauten Dessau*, 1930)

Der Architekt Walter Gropius war Gründer und erster Direktor des Bauhauses. Er nutzte die reformfreudige Atmosphäre und legte schon im April 1919 die bestehende Kunstakademie mit der Kunstgewerbeschule zum „Staatlichen Bauhaus Weimar" zusammen. Bei seinem Programm griff er auf die Ideen des revolutionären „Arbeitsrates für Kunst" zurück, die Ende 1918 unter der Leitung des Architekten Otto Bartning formuliert worden waren. Dazu gehörte vor allem die Auflösung der Schranken zwischen den künstlerischen Disziplinen Malerei, Bildhauerei und Architektur. Bauhaus – diesen Namen wählte Walter Gropius in Anlehnung an mittelalterliche Bauhütten. Wie beim Bau eines Domes sollten am Bauhaus Künstler, Handwerker und Architekten Hand in Hand arbeiten. Und mehr noch, eine gemeinsame Ausbildung war das Ziel.

Gropius holte in den folgenden Jahren die europäische Künstler-Avantgarde nach Weimar: Wassily Kandinsky, Paul Klee, Lyonel Feininger, László Moholy-Nagy, Oskar Schlemmer, Gerhard Marcks, Johannes Itten. Gemeinsam mit lokalen Handwerksmeistern leiteten sie die Ausbildung, die nach dem obligatorischen Vorkurs, einer Werkstattlehre und einer Architekturausbildung umfassend ausgebildete Gestalter hervorbringen sollte. Im Bauhaus-Manifest heißt es daher: „Das Endziel aller künstlerischen Tätigkeit ist der Bau."

Für den Anfang waren genügend Werkstätten vorhanden: Eine Weberei, Druckerei-, Metall- und Bildhauerwerkstatt, eine Buchbinderei, Glas- und Wandmalereiwerkstatt sowie eine Töpferei standen den Studierenden zur Verfügung. Einige der Werkstätten verschwanden mit der Zeit oder wurden umstrukturiert, andere kamen hinzu.

Der Unterricht am Weimarer Bauhaus war in seiner Formensprache noch stark vom Expressionismus geprägt. In den Werkstätten stand das handwerklich gefertigte Einzelstück im Vordergrund. Besonders Johannes Itten, der Schweizer Kunstpädagoge, war strikter Gegner einer Zusammenarbeit mit der Industrie. Dieses individuelle, handwerkliche Denken wurde nicht zuletzt durch den Einfluss des holländischen De Stijl-Künstlers Theo van Doesburg in Frage gestellt. Er unterrichtete zwar nicht direkt am Bauhaus, gab aber in Weimar Kurse und

Staatliches Bauhaus Weimar

The Bauhaus owes its nascence to a change of political climate in Europe. Germany lost the First World War, and Kaiser Wilhelm II abdicated in 1918. Berlin, the capital of the Reich, was still shaken by conflict, and so the new National Assembly convened in 1919 in Weimar. In August, the Weimar Reichsverfassung, or constitution, which was to pave the way for a new, democratic Germany, came into effect. A spirit of optimism ruled, particularly in the cultural sphere, and everything seemed possible.

"following the brutal interruption of work, which the war enforced, every thinking person was forced to re-adjust. Everyone longed to bridge the ominous dichotomy between reality and the mind from within his own field. the bauhaus became the reservoir for this intention". (Walter Gropius, *Bauhausbauten Dessau*, 1930).

The architect Walter Gropius was the founder and first director of the Bauhaus. He took advantage of the positive atmosphere of reform and, in April 1919, merged the existing art academy and school of arts and crafts to form the "Staatliches Bauhaus Weimar". His plans took up the concept of a revolutionary "work council" for art formulated by the architect Otto Bartning in 1918. This entailed, above all, the dissolution of the barriers between the artistic disciplines of painting, sculpture and architecture. Chosen by Walter Gropius, the name Bauhaus derives from a reference to the medieval builders' hut. At the Bauhaus, as with the construction of a cathedral, artists, crafts persons and architects were to work hand in hand. The goal, furthermore, was one of a shared learning process.

Over the following years, Gropius summoned the European avant-garde to Weimar: Wassily Kandinsky, Paul Klee, Lyonel Feininger, László Moholy-Nagy, Oskar Schlemmer, Gerhard Marcks and Johannes Itten. Together with local master craftsmen, these guided the educational process. This, with an obligatory preliminary course, a workshop apprenticeship and a course in architecture, was to yield extensively educated designers. Appropriately, the Bauhaus manifesto states "The ultimate goal of all artistic activity is the building".

To begin with, there were plenty of workshops: students had access to workshops for weaving, printing, metalwork, sculpture, bookbinding, glass and wall painting, as well as to a pottery. Some of the workshops disappeared or were restructured over time, while yet others were added.

Teaching at the Bauhaus in Weimar was, in terms of its formal language, still heavily influenced by Expressionism. In the workshops, the emphasis was on individual, handcrafted items. Johannes Itten in particular, the Swiss art teacher, was a vociferous opponent of collaboration with industry. This individual, crafts-orientated approach was questioned in no small part due to the influence of the Dutch De Stijl artist, Theo van Doesberg. Although not directly involved in teaching at the Bauhaus, van Doesberg held courses in Weimar, and made a great impression on the students there in 1922. In his view, the future of the designer did not lie in Expressionism, but in Constructivism, that is, not in the individual artwork, but in serial reproduction. In 1923, the Hungarian constructivist László Moholy-Nagy arrived at the Bauhaus. He described himself as an "artist engineer", and Gropius' new motto "Art and technology – a new unity" is strongly reflected in his work. Contemporary, industrial form design became the school's new field of activity. However, it became impossible to develop this activity further in Weimar. In 1924, the Bauhaus became a thorn in the side for the rightwing government elected in Thuringia. The alliance between a productive business and an educational establishment was one of the perceived problems, and, after a financial audit, they enforced a "precautionary" termination of employment contracts for March 31st 1925. When the Thuringian government halved the budget again, Gropius and the Bauhaus Masters' council announced the closure of the Staatliches Bauhaus Weimar in an open letter on 26th December 1924. (R. R. Isaacs, *Walter Gropius. Der Mensch und sein Werk*, 1983).

Bauhaus Dessau – School of Design

The school was meanwhile so well known that a number of cities, including Frankfurt am Main, Darmstadt, Hagen i. W. and Mannheim, were interested in taking it over. Ise Gropius even travelled through Germany in person to search for a new location, and spoke with, among others, the Lord Mayor of Cologne, Konrad Adenauer, who was soon taken with the idea of bringing the Bauhaus to the Rhineland. However, the so-called "Dance for the golden calf of the Bauhaus", as it was ironically labelled by Oskar Schlemmer, was finally won by the small city of Dessau in the Free State of Anhalt.

Dessau had a rich tradition of Enlightenment, and was the centre of the Dessau-Wörlitz Garden Realm, which was created in the late 18th century by Prince Franz von Anhalt-Dessau and the architect Friedrich von Erdmannsdorff. In the 1920s, Dessau became a burgeoning industrial town. The Junkers factory (which produced gas installations and built aircraft), the chemical industry and mechanical engineering concerns were among the many to settle here. The growth of these businesses was favoured by a brief period of economic prosperity in the mid-1920s.

The liberal Mayor Fritz Hesse (German Democratic Party) and the state conservation officer Ludwig Grote played a significant role in the decision to bring the Bauhaus to Dessau. Now a municipally funded institution, the school was renamed "Bauhaus Dessau – School of Design". The "Masters" of the Weimar period now became the school's professors. Hesse's great hope for the school was that it would provide an impetus for the construction of inexpensive social housing to supply the needs of the rapidly growing workforce. From 1925 to 1928, the population grew from 50,000 to 80,000.

Gropius not only valued the opportunity to work with industry, but also the generosity of the city's leaders, who provided one million Reichsmark for the construction of a new school building. Gropius' construction office was awarded contracts for the design of the Bauhaus Building, the Masters' Houses, the Törten Estate and, later on, the Employment Office in Dessau. Prior to the foundation of an independent department of

machte 1922 großen Eindruck auf die Schüler. Nicht im Expressionismus, sondern im Konstruktivismus – nicht im Einzelkunstwerk, sondern in der seriellen Produktion lag seiner Ansicht nach die Zukunft der Gestalter.

1923 kam der ungarische Konstruktivist László Moholy-Nagy ans Bauhaus. Er bezeichnete sich selbst als Künstler-Ingenieur, und Gropius' neues Motto „Kunst und Technik – eine neue Einheit" spiegelte sich besonders in seiner Arbeit wider. Zeitgerechte, industrielle Formgestaltung wurde zum neuen Arbeitsgebiet der Schule. In Weimar konnte sich diese Arbeit jedoch nicht mehr entfalten. Der 1924 gewählten deutsch-nationalen Regierung in Thüringen war das Bauhaus ein Dorn im Auge. Die Verknüpfung von Produktivbetrieb und Lehranstalt war eines der Probleme, und nach einer Finanzprüfung sprach sie eine „vorsorgliche" Kündigung der Arbeitsverträge zum 31. März 1925 aus. Nachdem darüber hinaus das Budget durch die Landesregierung halbiert worden war, gaben Gropius und der Meisterrat des Bauhauses am 26. Dezember 1924 in einem Offenen Brief die Auflösung des Staatlichen Bauhauses in Weimar bekannt. (R. R. Isaacs, *Walter Gropius. Der Mensch und sein Werk*, 1983)

Bauhaus Dessau – Hochschule für Gestaltung
Die Schule war inzwischen so bekannt, dass mehrere Städte an einer Übernahme interessiert waren, unter ihnen Frankfurt am Main, Darmstadt, Hagen i. W. und Mannheim. Ise Gropius reiste auf der Suche nach einem neuen Standort auch selbst durch Deutschland und sprach unter anderem mit dem Kölner Oberbürgermeister Konrad Adenauer, der bald von der Idee einer Übernahme des Bauhauses ins Rheinland angetan war. Den „Tanz um das goldene Kalb Bauhaus", wie Oskar Schlemmer es ironisch formulierte, gewann jedoch schließlich die kleine Stadt Dessau im Freistaat Anhalt.

Dessau war eine Stadt mit reicher aufklärerischer Tradition und Mittelpunkt des „Dessau-Wörlitzer Gartenreiches", das Ende des 18. Jahrhunderts von Fürst Franz von Anhalt-Dessau und dem Architekten Friedrich von Erdmannsdorff geschaffen worden war. In den 1920er Jahren entwickelte es sich zu einer aufstrebenden Industriestadt. Hier waren unter anderem die Junkers-Werke mit Gasgeräte- und Flugzeugbau, chemischer Industrie sowie Maschinenbau angesiedelt. Die kurze Zeit wirtschaftlicher Prosperität Mitte der 20er Jahre begünstigte die Entwicklung der Unternehmen.

Der liberale Bürgermeister Fritz Hesse (Deutsche Demokratische Partei) und Landeskonservator Ludwig Grote hatten maßgeblichen Anteil an der Entscheidung, das Bauhaus nach Dessau zu holen. Die Schule wurde zu einer kommunal finanzierten Einrichtung und hieß ab jetzt „Bauhaus Dessau – Hochschule für Gestaltung". Aus den „Meistern" der Weimarer Zeit wurden nun Hochschulprofessoren. Hesse versprach sich von der Schule vor allem Impulse für den sozialen Wohnungsbau, denn die schnell wachsende Arbeiterschaft brauchte preiswerten Wohnraum. Zwischen 1925 und 1928 stieg die Zahl der Einwohner von 50.000 auf 80.000 an.

Gropius schätzte nicht nur die Möglichkeit der Zusammenarbeit mit der Industrie, sondern auch die Großzügigkeit der Stadtväter, die eine Million Reichsmark für den Bau des neuen Schulgebäudes zur Verfügung stellten. Das Baubüro Gropius bekam den Auftrag zum Entwurf des Bauhausgebäudes, der Meisterhäuser, der Siedlung Törten und später auch des Arbeitsamtes in Dessau. Bis zur Einrichtung einer eigenen Bauabteilung 1927 fungierte das Büro auch als Ausbildungsstätte für Bauhäusler.

1928 legte Gropius nach Jahren des aufreibenden Einsatzes für die Schule sein Amt nieder, um sich verstärkt wieder seinen eigenen Architekturplanungen zu widmen. Als Nachfolger schlug er den Schweizer Architekten Hannes Meyer vor, der ein Jahr zuvor die Bauabteilung des Bauhauses begründet hatte. In Abgrenzung zu Gropius stellte er soziale über künstlerische Fragen. Im Vordergrund stand der Entwurf preiswerter, praktischer Möbel, und das neue Motto hieß „Volksbedarf statt Luxusbedarf". Nach seiner Berufung stellte Meyer das Studium auf eine breitere wissenschaftliche Basis, und die Werkstätten arbeiteten so profitabel wie noch nie. Die Zusammenarbeit mit der Industrie wurde forciert, die Lizenzeinnahmen stiegen. Die Erfolge des Bauhauses waren selten so sichtbar wie in der Zeit zwischen 1928 und 1930, und Meyer konnte ernten, was in den Jahren zuvor vorbereitet worden war. Dennoch war dieses „rote Bauhaus", wie es im Volksmund aufgrund der aktiven Kommunistischen Studentenfraktion genannt wurde, den Stadträten nicht genehm. Hannes Meyer wurde im Herbst 1930 von der Stadt fristlos entlassen, bevor die Rufe nach einer Schließung der Schule zu laut wurden.

Sein Nachfolger Ludwig Mies van der Rohe war zu dieser Zeit einer der bekanntesten Architekten im Deutschen Reich. Er hatte sich mit der Weißenhof-Siedlung in Stuttgart 1927 und dem Deutschen Pavillon auf der Weltausstellung in Barcelona 1929 einen Namen gemacht. Die Stadtväter beauftragten ihn, die Arbeit am Bauhaus zu entideologisieren. Eine politische Betätigung wurde untersagt, die studentische Mitbestimmung eingeschränkt und radikale Studierende der Schule verwiesen. Inhaltlich formte Mies das Bauhaus stärker zu einer Architekturschule um, denn Gropius' Idee der Einheit von bildender Kunst, Handwerk und Baukunst teilte er nur bedingt.

Trotz aller Bemühungen wurde das Bauhaus Dessau zwei Jahre später auf Antrag der Nationalsozialisten im Stadtrat geschlossen. Nur die kommunistischen Abgeordneten und Oberbürgermeister Hesse stimmten dagegen, die SPD enthielt sich aus wahltaktischen Gründen. Mies erreichte immerhin eine Fortzahlung der Lehrergehälter. So konnte das Bauhaus wenigstens für kurze Zeit als privates Institut in Berlin weiterarbeiten.

architecture in 1927, the office also served as a training centre for students at the Bauhaus.

In 1928, following years of gruelling work, Gropius resigned from the school in order to dedicate more time to his own architectural plans. He proposed the Swiss architect Hannes Meyer, who had established the department of architecture at the Bauhaus the year before, as his successor. Meyer differed from Gropius in that he prioritised social, rather than artistic, issues. The focus was put on the design of inexpensive and practical furniture, and the new motto was *Volksbedarf statt Luxusbedarf*, or "People's needs vs. luxury goods". Following his appointment, Meyer established the curriculum on a broader scientific basis, and the workshops became more profitable than ever. Collaboration with industry was promoted, and the revenue from licence agreements grew. The successes of the Bauhaus were rarely as evident as they were between 1928 and 1930, and Meyer was able to reap the rewards of the previous years' work. Nevertheless, this "Red Bauhaus" – so-called due to the active Communist student faction – became inconvenient for the city council. In 1930, Hannes Meyer was summarily dismissed by the city council before calls for the school's closure became too vociferous.

His successor, Ludwig Mies van der Rohe, was then one of the best-known architects in the German Reich, having made a name for himself with the Weißenhof Estate in Stuttgart in 1927 and the German Pavilion at the Barcelona World Fair in 1929. The city's leaders ordered him to purge all ideological aspects from work at the Bauhaus. Political activity was prohibited, student participation was circumscribed, and radical students were expelled from the school. In terms of content, Mies reformed the Bauhaus along the lines of a more conventional architectural school, because he only shared Gropius' concept of the unity of art, crafts and architecture to a limited degree.

Despite all efforts, the Bauhaus in Dessau was closed two years later at the behest of the National Socialist members of the city council. Only the communist delegates and Lord Mayor Hesse voted against; the SPD declined to vote for tactical reasons. Mies, however, managed to ensure that the teachers still received their salaries. In this way, the Bauhaus was, at least for a brief period, able to continue as a private institute in Berlin.

Bauhaus Berlin In October 1932, the Bauhaus moved to a disused telephone factory in Berlin-Steglitz. Financed by private subsidies and revenues from licence agreements, it was now called the Freies Lehr- und Forschungsinstitut. For Mies van der Rohe, the emphasis was again very clearly on architecture: "It is our aim to educate architects in such a way that they have a command of the entire field of architecture, from the construction of individual houses to town planning. This would not only include the design of the actual building, but also the design of all the furnishing, even the textiles." (*Steglitzer Anzeiger*, October 1932)

However, practical work at the Bauhaus in Berlin continued for just a few months. By late January 1933, the National Socialists had assumed power across the German Reich. In April of the same year, the prosecuting authorities had the new premises searched for material incriminating the Lord Mayor, Fritz Hesse. The Secret State Police, or Gestapo, then sealed off the building.

In the following weeks, Mies and the Masters and students tried in vain to reopen the school. Should it have enabled work to continue, Mies van der Rohe was even prepared to meet the political demands made subsequently by the National Socialist government, including the dismissal of Wassily Kandinsky and Ludwig Hilberseimer. In the meantime, however, all payments of salaries had been suspended, making work impossible. Worn down by economic constraints and political unpredictability, the Bauhaus Masters decided, at their last meeting in July 1933, to close the school for the last time.

Bauhaus Berlin Im Oktober 1932 siedelte das Bauhaus in eine stillgelegte Telefonfabrik nach Berlin-Steglitz über. Finanziert durch private Zuschüsse und Lizenzeinnahmen hieß es nun „Freies Lehr- und Forschungsinstitut". Für Mies van der Rohe stand auch hier ganz klar die Architektur im Vordergrund: „Unser Ziel ist, Architekten so auszubilden, daß sie das ganze Gebiet, das in die Architektur hineinreicht, beherrschen, vom Kleinwohnungsbau bis zum Städtebau, nicht nur den eigentlichen Bau, sondern auch die gesamte Einrichtung bis hinab zu den Textilien." (*Steglitzer Anzeiger*, Oktober 1932)

Zur praktischen Arbeit kam das Bauhaus in Berlin aber nur noch wenige Monate. Ende Januar 1933 hatten die Nationalsozialisten reichsweit die Macht übernommen, und im April des Jahres ließ die Staatsanwaltschaft das neue Domizil auf belastendes Material gegen Oberbürgermeister Fritz Hesse durchsuchen. Das Gebäude wurde anschließend von der Geheimen Staatspolizei (Gestapo) versiegelt.

In den folgenden Wochen versuchten Mies, die Meister und die Studierenden vergeblich, die Schule wieder zu öffnen. Den schließlich formulierten politischen Forderungen der nationalsozialistischen Regierung, unter anderem der Entlassung von Wassily Kandinsky und Ludwig Hilberseimer, hätte Mies van der Rohe sogar zugestimmt, um eine Weiterarbeit zu ermöglichen. Inzwischen waren jedoch die Lohnzahlungen eingestellt worden, was eine Fortsetzung der Arbeit unmöglich machte. Aufgerieben zwischen wirtschaftlichen Zwängen und politischen Unwägbarkeiten, beschlossen die Meister des Bauhauses in ihrer letzten Sitzung im Juli 1933, die Schule endgültig aufzulösen.

The Bauhaus Building in Dessau
Das Bauhausgebäude in Dessau

Einführung

Introduction

"When I saw the 'Bauhaus', the whole of which seems to have been cast in one piece like a persistent thought, and its glass walls, which create a transparent corner that merges into the air but is nevertheless separated from it by a precise will – I stopped, involuntarily, in my tracks (…)". The Russian author Ilja Ehrenburg was evidently impressed by his visit to the Bauhaus in 1927. This citation is of interest as historic evidence, as it describes the Bauhaus as we no longer see it today: a gleaming white, otherworldly building, built on the proverbial green lawn, and visible from afar. This was an unusual sight for society in the 1920s, as its colossal glass façade and provocative formal language made it unique. Industrially manufactured building materials, new methods of construction and abstract forms – the combination of these elements means that the building still looks timelessly modern today.

By now, the Bauhaus is surrounded by other buildings, and can barely be seen from afar. It therefore may seem smaller, not quite as if cast in one piece, and less majestic than in the historical photos. The structure of reinforced concrete and glass, rendered brickwork and rows of windows has long become standard in construction and design terms, and many of its functional aspects have been superseded. One needs some knowledge of early 20th century (architectural) history, and a love of detail, to recognise the salient features of this thoroughly interesting building.

The Bauhaus Building in Dessau was built in 1925/26 to Walter Gropius' design, and is seen today as a built manifestation both of the Bauhaus concept and of philanthropic Modernism. It was commissioned by the city of Dessau for two separate schools, the Bauhaus Dessau – School of Design and the municipal vocational school. Engineering and trades apprentices and international avant-garde artists therefore found themselves under one roof.

The building is subdivided into three wings: the workshop tract, the studio building and the north wing. At the time, the workshop tract (with the glass curtain wall) was where the Bauhaus' practical experiments were carried out. Its four floors accommodated the carpentry, the textile workshop, the metal workshop, the workshop for printing and advertising, the wall painting classes and later also the photography workshop. The adjoining building, likewise part of the Bauhaus, included the auditorium, the stage and the canteen. The rooms in this so-called "festive area" have the same kind of windows throughout, so that it appears, from outside, to be a self-contained part of the building. Only when inside does one become aware of its diverse functions, colours and fittings. The studio building rises above the kitchen at the eastern end of the festive area. At the time, this residential block had 28 rooms for students. The rehearsal rooms for the theatre workshop were located underneath the stage.

The bridge linked the School of Design with the municipal vocational school and traversed Leopolddank street (now Bauhausstraße). The second floor of the bridge initially housed Walter Gropius' building office, although the newly established department of architecture directed by Hannes Meyer moved

„Als ich das ‚Bauhaus' erblickte, das ganz aus einem Stück gegossen zu sein scheint wie ein beharrlicher Gedanke, und seine Glaswände, die einen durchsichtigen Winkel bilden, mit der Luft verfließend und doch von ihr getrennt durch einen exakten Willen – da blieb ich unwillkürlich stehen […]." Der russische Schriftsteller Ilja Ehrenburg war sichtlich beeindruckt bei seinem Besuch des Bauhauses im Jahr 1927. Dieses Zitat ist interessant als Zeitzeugnis, denn es beschreibt das Bauhausgebäude, wie wir es heute nicht mehr erleben können: ein weiß leuchtender Bau wie aus einer anderen Welt, sprichwörtlich auf der grünen Wiese gebaut und schon von weitem sichtbar. Eine ungewohnte Erscheinung für die Menschen in den 20er Jahren, einzigartig mit seiner riesigen Glasfassade und provokativ in der Formensprache. Industriell verarbeitete Baustoffe, neue Konstruktionsweisen, abstrakte Formen – die Kombination dieser Elemente lässt den Bau auch heute noch zeitlos modern erscheinen.

Heute ist das Bauhaus von allen Seiten umbaut und kaum noch aus der Distanz zu betrachten. Vielleicht wirkt es deshalb kleiner, nicht gerade wie aus einem Guss und weniger majestätisch als auf historischen Fotos. Der Bau aus Stahlbeton und Glas, aus verputztem Ziegelmauerwerk und zahlreichen Fensterbändern ist heute konstruktiv sowie gestalterisch längst Standard und an vielen Stellen funktional überholt. Man braucht eine gewisse Kenntnis der (Architektur-) Geschichte des frühen 20. Jahrhunderts und Liebe zum Detail, um sich die Besonderheiten dieses überaus interessanten Gebäudes zu vergegenwärtigen.

Das Bauhausgebäude in Dessau wurde 1925/26 nach einem Entwurf von Walter Gropius errichtet und gilt heute sowohl als gebautes Manifest der Bauhaus-Idee als auch einer menschenfreundlichen Moderne. Es wurde im Auftrag der Stadt Dessau für zwei unterschiedliche Schulen errichtet, die Hochschule für Gestaltung – Bauhaus Dessau und die Gewerbliche Berufsschule der Stadt. So fanden die Lehrlinge aus Handwerk und Technik und die internationale künstlerische Avantgarde Platz unter einem Dach.

Der Bau gliedert sich in drei Flügel: den Werkstättentrakt, das Ateliergebäude und den Nordflügel. Im Werkstättentrakt mit der Glasvorhangfassade fand damals die praktische Versuchsarbeit des Bauhauses statt. Die Tischlerei, die Weberei, die Metallwerkstatt, die Werkstatt für Druck und Reklame, die Wandmalereiklasse und später auch die Werkstatt für Fotografie waren hier auf vier Geschossen untergebracht. Ebenfalls zum Bauhaus gehörte der von den Werkstätten aus erreichbare Zwischenbau mit Aula, Bühne und Kantine. Die Räume dieser so genannten Festebene haben durchgehend die gleichen Fenster, so dass der Zwischenbau von außen wie ein in sich geschlossener Gebäudeteil wirkt. Erst im Innern erkennt man die Vielfalt der Nutzung, der Farbigkeit und der Ausstattung. Über der Küche am östlichen Ende der Festebene schließlich erhebt sich das Ateliergebäude als Wohnturm, mit damals 28 Zimmern für die Studierenden. Unter der Bühne waren die Proberäume für die Theaterwerkstatt untergebracht. Die Brücke verband die Hochschule für Gestaltung mit der Städtischen Berufsschule und überspannte den Leopolddank (heute Bauhausstraße). Im oberen Geschoss der Brücke befand sich zunächst das Baubüro von Walter Gropius, 1927 zog hier die neu gegründete Bau-

in in 1927. The lower floor of the bridge housed the administrative departments for both schools, with the Bauhaus director's room occupying the centre of the building.

Opposite the workshop tract, in the north wing, as many students were taught per year in the rooms of the then vocational school as there were in the Bauhaus during its entire existence. Gropius designed this tract less spectacularly than the rest of the building, owing to its function as a traditional school consisting only of classrooms and rooms for administration purposes.

There is no central view of the Bauhaus, but, for that, there are a number of entrances, which emphasise the building's various functions. One must circle the building to fully appreciate the individually designed cubes and their purposes. These cubes reflect Gropius' idea of a "large-scale set of 'building blocks'", i.e., independently functional building elements that intersect one another, yet form an aesthetic unity. In the interior of the building, which can easily confuse the visitor with its two large staircases and four storeys, other principles come to the fore: the interplay of light and shadow, of symmetry and asymmetry, and of intersecting pathways and visual axes. The aim was to encourage the user's conscious perception of spatial principles, construction, colour and materiality, and these aspects continue to make the architecture exciting and dynamic today.

The famous Bauhaus lettering, which uses capital letters, is found on the southwesterly corner of the building. At the time, the area was closed off from the south, and this was the first thing that visitors to the Bauhaus would see. Even from afar, the school, in a period where advertising was on the increase, confidently used block letters to attract attention. It is also possible, from this location, to perceive the building's integration within the urban landscape. The workshop wing is set back from the street in answer to the open area opposite, which was also an integral part of the original plans. During the National Socialist era, houses built in the traditional Heimatschutz style were built here in deliberate opposition to the avant-garde architecture of the Weimar Republic.

The Bauhaus Building was erected within a brief construction period of just one year. The liberal use of new building materials such as reinforced concrete and glass and its skeleton construction in fact made it one of the most modern buildings of its time. The glass curtain wall in particular was, in its size and aesthetic character, unique for its time. Not only the building envelope, but also the colours and the furnishings were, for Gropius, integral parts of the design. These were developed and realised in the school's workshops, thereby integrating the Bauhaus students in the realisation of the Gesamtkunstwerk. Concept, architecture and design create a homogenous unit.

abteilung unter Hannes Meyer ein. Im unteren Geschoss der Brücke saß die Administration beider Schulen, mit dem Direktorenzimmer des Bauhauses als Zentrum des Gebäudes.

Gegenüber dem Werkstättentrakt, im Nordflügel, wurden in den Räumen der damaligen Gewerblichen Berufsschule pro Jahr so viele Schüler unterrichtet wie im Bauhaus während seines ganzen Bestehens. Gropius gestaltete diesen Trakt weniger spektakulär als den Rest des Gebäudes, geschuldet seiner Funktion als traditionellem Schulbau mit Lehr- und Verwaltungsräumen.

Eine zentrale Ansicht des Bauhausgebäudes gibt es nicht, dafür viele Eingänge, die die unterschiedlichen Funktionen des Baus unterstreichen. Man muss um das Gebäude herumgehen, um die individuell gestalteten Kuben und ihre Nutzung zu erfassen. Sie spiegeln das von Gropius entwickelte Prinzip des „Baukastens im Großen" wider, d.h. einzeln funktionierender Gebäudeteile, die ineinander geschachtelt sind und doch eine ästhetische Einheit ergeben. Im Innern des Gebäudes, das den Besucher durch seine zwei großen Treppenhäuser und vier Geschosse leicht verwirren kann, werden noch andere Prinzipien deutlich: das Spiel mit Licht und Schatten, mit Symmetrie und Asymmetrie sowie mit Weg- und Sichtachsen. Die bewusste Wahrnehmung von raumbildenden Prinzipien, von Konstruktion, Farbe und Materialität durch die Nutzer war erwünscht und macht die Architektur bis heute spannend und lebendig.

An der Südwestecke des Gebäudes befindet sich der berühmte Bauhaus-Schriftzug in Blockbuchstaben. Damals war das Areal von Süden her erschlossen, und wer das Bauhaus besuchte, sah diese Ansicht als erste. Schon von weitem machte die Schule in einer Zeit zunehmender Reklame mit großen Lettern selbstbewusst auf sich aufmerksam. Von diesem Standort aus lässt sich auch die städtebauliche Einbindung des Gebäudes gut erkennen. Der Werkstattflügel ist aus der Straßenflucht zurückgesetzt und antwortet so auf den gegenüberliegenden Platz, der damals bereits vorgesehen war. Während des Nationalsozialismus wurden hier in bewusster Opposition zum Avantgarde-Bau der demokratischen Weimarer Republik Wohnhäuser im so genannten Heimatschutzstil errichtet.

Das Bauhausgebäude wurde in der kurzen Bauzeit von nur einem Jahr errichtet. Die großzügige Verwendung neuer Baustoffe wie Stahlbeton und Glas sowie die Konstruktion als Skelettbau machten es tatsächlich zu einem der modernsten Bauten seiner Zeit. Besonders die Glasvorhangfassade war in ihrer Größe und Ästhetik damals einmalig. Aber nicht nur die Gebäudehülle selbst, auch die Farbigkeit sowie die Innenausstattung waren für Gropius Bestandteile des Entwurfs. Sie wurden in den eigenen Schulwerkstätten entwickelt und realisiert und banden so die Bauhausschüler in die Realisation des Gesamtkunstwerkes ein. Idee, Architektur und Gestaltung bilden eine untrennbare Einheit.

Festive area

The ground floor entrance area was both a reception area and a vantage point for visitors to the building. In 1926, one had an extensive and unspoilt view through the large, undivided glass sheets. When the auditorium doors are open, the reflections from the four mirrors on the right-hand wall turn the area into a Baroque spatial axis. Here, the entrance area, auditorium, stage and canteen interlock to create the festive area.

The three large double-doors attract our attention by means of their glossy varnish and semi-circular nickel-plated handles, which, when the doors are closed, form complete circles. Sections of the door recesses also have a glossy finish, and the door grips are distinctive: the hemispherical auditorium door handles fit exactly into circular hollows in the partition walls. This is a design 'trick', which Gropius may have adopted from the nearby Schloss Wörlitz, built by Fürst Franz, which uses a similar principle. The colour design is by László Moholy-Nagy. The doors, bright alcoves, pink wall, large window and mirrors dominate the entrance area in terms of colour and light, as the (in part) dark blue finish on the ceiling recesses is only seen at a second glance.

Owing to its asymmetric alignment, the lighting system leads the visitor towards the auditorium and seems to continue beyond the wall from there. The student Max Krajewski designed the system especially for this room. The tubular bulbs are bare – no shades, no decors. The lights in the auditorium under the silver, light-reflecting ceiling are also highly decorative, and although they appear to have been mass-produced, the frames were actually made by hand. The lighting was at all events provocative, as was the whole room, which was used as an auditorium for plays and concerts, and at first glance lacked any similarity to the traditional, representational theatre architecture.

The auditorium and stage formed an important communal centre within the Bauhaus. Here, festivals were celebrated, concerts were held, and experimental, abstract plays by Oskar Schlemmer and his students, including pieces such as the stick, form and hoop dances, were rehearsed.

The furniture was designed in the carpentry workshop, and it was here that design history was made: The tubular steel seating was the first of its kind worldwide. Inspired by the aluminium seats designed in Dessau for the Junkers aircraft, Marcel Breuer ultimately made metal furniture presentable. Legend has it that Breuer's tubular steel designs were also inspired by the handlebars on his new bicycle. Today, however, the original rows of nickel-plated tubular steel seats are no longer in situ. They have been destroyed during the times and have been replaced by facsimiles in 1992.

In the year 1926, the original upholstery was made of a conventional cotton material – a type of sailcloth. In the late 1920s, this was replaced by a Bauhaus invention called Eisengarn (literally, iron yarn), which was developed by artists in the textile workshop especially for the new tubular steel furniture. This double-yarn, specially impregnated textile earned its name due to its shine, strength and durability – iron yarn was not actually woven into the textile. In 2004, during the renovation process,

Festebene

Das Vestibül im Erdgeschoss war für die Besucher Empfangsbereich und Aussichtsplattform zugleich. Durch die großen, ungeteilten Glasscheiben hatte man 1926 einen weiten, unverstellten Blick. Die vier Spiegel rechts an der Wand lassen bei geöffneten Aulatüren den Bereich zu einer barocken Raumachse werden, und hier verschränken sich der Eingangsbereich, die Aula, die Bühne und die Mensa zur Festebene.

Die drei großen Flügeltüren fallen durch ihre glänzende Lackierung und die vernickelten Beschläge auf, die sich zu Kreisen ergänzen. Auch Teile der Türnischen sind glänzend gefasst, und eine Besonderheit sind die Griffmulden: Die Halbkugeln der Aulatürgriffe passen exakt in die Mulden der Zwischenwände. Ein gestalterischer Trick, den sich Gropius im nahen Wörlitzer Schloss des Fürsten Franz abgeschaut haben mag, wo es ein ähnliches Prinzip gibt. Die Farbgebung stammt von László Moholy-Nagy. Die Türen, die hellen Nischen, eine rosafarbene Wand, das große Fenster und die Spiegel dominieren das Vestibül farb- und lichttechnisch, die teils tiefblau gefassten Deckennischen entdeckt man erst auf den zweiten Blick.

Das Leuchtensystem lenkt durch seine asymmetrische Position den Besucher in Richtung der Aula und scheint sich dort hinter der Wand fortzusetzen. Der Student Max Krajewski aus der Metallwerkstatt entwarf es speziell für diese Räume. Die Soffitten liegen frei – kein Schirm, kein Schnörkel ziert sie. Auch die Leuchten in der Aula unter der silbernen, das Licht reflektierenden Decke stellen ein stark dekoratives Element dar. Sie scheinen seriell produziert zu sein, tatsächlich wurden die Gestänge aber einzeln gefertigt, und nur die Soffitten waren damals schon Industrieprodukte. Eine Provokation waren sie ohnehin, wie der ganze Raum, der auch als Zuschauerraum für Bühnenstücke und Konzerte fungierte und auf den ersten Blick jede Ähnlichkeit mit traditioneller, repräsentativer Theaterarchitektur vermissen ließ.

Die Aula mit der Bühne war ein wichtiges gemeinschaftliches Zentrum innerhalb des Bauhauses. Hier wurden Feste gefeiert, Konzerte gegeben und die experimentellen, abstrakten Bühnenstücke Oskar Schlemmers und seiner Studierenden geprobt, zum Beispiel Tanztheaterstücke wie der Stäbe-, Formen- oder Reifentanz.

Das Mobiliar wurde in der Tischlereiwerkstatt entworfen, und hier wurde Designgeschichte geschrieben: das Stahlrohrreihengestühl war das erste seiner Art weltweit. Marcel Breuer machte Metallmöbel salonfähig, inspiriert durch Aluminiumsitze, wie sie für Junkers-Flugzeuge in Dessau entwickelt worden waren. Der Legende nach regte auch der Lenker seines neuen Fahrrades Breuer zu seinen Entwürfen aus Metallrohr an. Zu sehen sind heute allerdings nicht mehr die originalen Stuhlreihen aus vernickeltem Stahlrohr, sondern ein originalgetreuer Nachbau von 1992.

Die Stoffbespannung war 1926 zunächst ein herkömmliches Baumwollgewebe, eine Art Segeltuch. Ende der 20er Jahre wurde es durch eine Bauhaus-Erfindung ersetzt, das Eisengarngewebe, eigens von den Künstlerinnen der Textilwerkstatt für die neuen Stahlrohrmöbel entworfen. Das doppelt gezwirnte, speziell imprägnierte Gewebe erhielt seinen Namen wegen seines Glanzes, seiner Festigkeit und Haltbarkeit – Metallfäden sind nicht darin verwoben.

the original cotton textile dating from 1926 was replicated and re-fitted.

Black folding doors separate the stage from the Bauhaus canteen, and not from a backstage area – creating an unusual and unique sequence of rooms. Today, this is a public refectory, accessible from the stairs leading to the studio building. It is popular with visitors, students at the neighbouring Anhalt University and the Bauhaus' employees, and has room now, as then, for 90 covers. It is furnished with the B9 stool, likewise designed by Marcel Breuer. The issue of whether the B9 is an artwork or a utility object has occupied legal experts since 2001, as a number of manufacturers have disputed the reproduction rights. Despite the judicial finding, which defined the stool as an artwork, in historic terms the B9 is a utility object, albeit one with an artistic value. The stool combines many elements also evident in other pieces of furniture by Marcel Breuer: using few parts and limited materials, they are simple, elegant, multifunctional and suitable for industrial reproduction. These characteristics also apply to Breuer's canteen tables, which, with their cubic form, flush quadrangular legs and finely polished varnished surface, have a timeless, elegant look. The furniture in the canteen consists of facsimiles dating from 1994. The kitchen is connected to the canteen via an exceptionally large serving hatch. This 'transparency' was designed so that one could see the work carried out in the kitchen, thus providing a control facility and ensuring the hygienic preparation of food.

A look at the canteen ceiling reveals the great importance ascribed to the surfaces in the Bauhaus Building. Rough plaster was applied to the two outer areas, and another, smoother plaster in the central zone, creating a type of reflected ceiling plan. The beams are coated with a dark matt paint on the sides and a light, glossy paint on the undersides so that they respond to the reflection of light from the dining tables. The colour concept in the canteen was designed in the school's wall painting workshop, and its bright red-orange is truly astonishing. It is shown off to its best advantage in artificial light, which allows the room to appear friendly by night. The three hemispherical lights were designed by Max Krajewski. These flood the room with light and are, bar a few original elements, facsimiles. The four vertically aligned casement windows may be opened and closed by turning a wheel. In this way, two or three rows of windows, that is, eight to ten casements may be opened simultaneously and fixed in any position. Despite the permanent draught in the Bauhaus, these windows do not slam because they are all fitted with adjustable locking mechanisms.

2004 wurde im Rahmen der Sanierung das ursprüngliche Baumwollgewebe von 1926 rekonstruiert und aufgezogen.

Schwarze Falttüren trennen die Bühne nicht etwa von einem Kulissenraum, sondern von der Bauhaus-Kantine – eine ungewöhnliche und einzigartige Raumfolge. Heute ist diese wochentags eine öffentliche Mensa, erreichbar über die Treppe zum Ateliergebäude. Sie wird gern von Besuchern, Studierenden der benachbarten Hochschule Anhalt sowie den Bauhaus-Angestellten selbst genutzt und bietet heute wie damals 90 Essern Platz. Ausgestattet ist sie mit dem Hocker B9, ebenfalls ein Entwurf Marcel Breuers. Mit der Frage, ob der B9 ein Kunstwerk oder ein Gebrauchsgegenstand sei, haben sich seit 2001 Juristen auseinandergesetzt, denn verschiedene Herstellerfirmen machten sich das Recht zur Reproduktion streitig. Trotz der gerichtlichen Deklaration als Kunstwerk ist der B9 historisch betrachtet ein Gebrauchsgegenstand – mit künstlerischem Wert. Der Hocker vereint viele Elemente, die sich auch bei anderen Möbeln Breuers finden: aus nur wenigen Teilen und Materialien bestehend, schlicht, elegant, multifunktional und maschinenproduzierbar, ebenso Breuers Mensa-Tische. Die Holztische mit ihrer kubischen Form, ihren bündig angesetzten, viereckigen Beinen und der edlen Schleiflackoberfläche wirken zeitlos elegant. Die Möbel in der Mensa wurden 1994 nachgebaut. An den Speisesaal schließt die Küche mit der ungewöhnlich großen Durchreiche an. Diese Transparenz sollte den Arbeitsprozess sichtbar machen und durch diese Kontrollmöglichkeit eine hygienische Essenszubereitung sicherstellen.

Ein Blick unter die Decke der Mensa zeigt, welcher hohe Stellenwert den Oberflächen im Bauhaus beigemessen wurde. Rauer Putz wurde in den beiden Außenzonen, unterschiedlich glatter Putz in der Mittelzone verwendet, wodurch eine Art Deckenspiegel entsteht. Die Unterzüge sind seitlich matt dunkel, aber unten hell glänzend lackiert und antworten auf die Lichtreflexionen der Esstische. Das Farbkonzept der Mensa wurde in der Wandmalereiwerkstatt der Schule entworfen und überrascht durch sein leuchtendes Rot-Orange. Dieses kommt besonders bei künstlichem Licht zur Geltung und lässt den Raum auch bei Dunkelheit freundlich erscheinen. Max Krajewski entwarf die drei Schalenleuchten, die den Raum voll ausleuchten und bis auf wenige originale Einzelteile ebenfalls Nachbauten sind.

Bemerkenswert sind die Fensteröffnungsmechanismen. Durch das Drehen eines Rades setzt man die vier vertikal angeordneten Fensterflügel in Bewegung. Auf diese Weise können zwei bzw. drei Fensterbänder, also acht bis zwölf Fensterflügel gleichzeitig geöffnet und in jeder beliebigen Position gehalten werden. Zuschlagende Fenster gibt es trotz der permanenten Zugluft im Bauhaus nicht, weil alle Mechanismen eine flexible Arretierung erlauben.

Staircases and bridge The large staircases of both schools and the bridge that linked them were the most important public spaces in the building. No one could move through this transparent construction unseen, and these were the most important axes in the building. They reflected the dynamism of the schools, and are still used as the main routes through the Bauhaus today.

The windows, lights and radiators stand at the centre of attention. The idea of the vaulted rotating windows in the stairwells derives from the industrial architecture of the 19th century. With the aid of a chain, several windows may be opened simultaneously, and the effect is astonishing: the dark patterns created by the opening casements join forces with the sky to create a moving, graphic display. The motto "Art and technology – a new unity" is reflected in architectural form; functionality and design are palpably united. Here, Gropius also incorporated technical elements usually associated with galleries, and the deliberate sophistication of the technology shows the great importance of the art of engineering within the architecture.

The staircases are lit by spherical lights designed by Marianne Brandt for the Bauhaus Building in 1926, when she was a student in the metal workshop. Many of them were also found in the classrooms and offices. Only a few original examples of these are left in the building. The matt glass sphere appears to have been put together from two parts, but is made in one piece. The lower, slightly larger piece is coated with a milky opal glass to ensure the optimal indirect lighting for work. The fact that the lamp appears to consist of two parts is mainly due to practical, rather than aesthetic, reasons: the overlay of opal glass resulted in flaws that were concealed by the increase in thickness. In 1930, in his book *Bauhausbauten Dessau*, Gropius introduced this lamp by quoting, with tongue in cheek, Karl Friedrich Schinkel: "Make a virtue of the join!", i.e., link functionality and design as skilfully as possible.

The hemispherical lights in the foyers on the first and second floors were designed by Max Krajewski. These are very similar to those in the canteen in that they also consist of a hemispherical element hanging from a three-legged frame, and of black glass combined with white. These are complemented by the cylindrical lights by Marianne Brandt, which are found in both of the corridors on the bridge. These corridors are accessed from the staircases and link the workshop tract with the north wing.

On the lower level of the bridge, a number of offices stand in a row. The public corridor juts out without support, and there are no concrete stanchions interrupting the long row of windows, which is outlined by a stripe of red paint. This guides the visitor over the bridge, and draws attention to the outside, where real axes (pathways) and sight axes intersect. The lights are concealed between the beams and do not distract from the spatial alignment of the corridor. The window opening mechanisms are inconspicuous, and small windows above and below may be opened like a skylight or downwards onto the windowsill. During the renovation, the larger, opening windows were also reconstructed; these allow the space to be aired quickly.

Treppenhäuser und Brücke Die wichtigsten öffentlichen Räume des Gebäudes waren die großen Treppenhäuser beider Schulen und die sie verbindende Brücke. Niemand konnte sich hier ungesehen durch den transparenten Bau bewegen, es waren die wichtigsten Achsen des Hauses. Hier zeigte sich die Dynamik der Schulen, und bis heute sind dies die zentralen Wege im Bauhaus.

Im Mittelpunkt der Aufmerksamkeit stehen die Fenster, Leuchten und Heizkörper. Die Idee der gekuppelten Drehfenster in den Treppenhäusern entstammt der Industriearchitektur des 19. Jahrhunderts. Mittels einer Kette lassen sich mehrere Flügel gleichzeitig öffnen, und der Effekt ist erstaunlich: Die dunkle Struktur der sich öffnenden Fensterflügel wirkt gegen den Himmel wie eine bewegliche Grafik. Das Motto „Kunst und Technik – eine neue Einheit" zeigt sich hier in gebauter Form, Funktionalität und Gestaltung sind augenfällig vereint. Gropius inszenierte an dieser Stelle zudem technische Elemente wie in einer Galerie, und die bewusste Nobilitierung der Technik zeigt den hohen Stellenwert der Ingenieurskunst innerhalb der Architektur.

Beleuchtet werden die Treppenhäuser durch Kugelleuchten von Marianne Brandt. Die Studentin der Metallwerkstatt entwarf sie 1926 für das Bauhausgebäude, und sie hingen in großer Zahl auch in den Lehrsälen und Büros. Von ihnen gibt es nur noch wenige bauzeitliche Exemplare im Haus. Die Kugel aus Mattglas wirkt wie aus zwei Teilen zusammengesetzt, ist aber aus einem Stück gefertigt. Der untere, etwas größere Teil ist mit milchigem Opalglas überzogen und soll ein optimales, indirektes Arbeitslicht gewährleisten. Dass die Lampe optisch zweigeteilt wirkt, hatte weniger ästhetische als praktische Gründe. Das Überfangen mit Opalglas brachte Ungenauigkeiten mit sich, die durch die Verdickung kaschiert wurden. In seinem Buch *Bauhausbauten Dessau* stellte Gropius 1930 diese Lampe vor und zitierte dazu mit einem Augenzwinkern Karl Friedrich Schinkel: „Aus der Naht eine Tugend machen!", d.h. Funktionalität und Gestaltung auf möglichst geschickte Weise verbinden.

Die Schalenleuchten in den Foyers im ersten und zweiten Obergeschoss wurden von Max Krajewski gestaltet. Sie ähneln stark denen in der Mensa, denn auch hier ist ein hängendes Kugelsegment mit einem dreibeinigen Gestänge, schwarzes Glas mit weißem kombiniert. Sie werden ergänzt durch die zylindrischen Leuchten von Marianne Brandt, die sich auch auf beiden Brückengängen befinden. Diese werden durch die Treppenhäuser erschlossen und verbinden den Werkstättentrakt mit dem Nordflügel.

Auf der unteren Brücke reiht sich ein Büro an das nächste. Der öffentliche Gang kragt stützenlos aus, kein Betonpfeiler unterbricht das lange Fensterband, das von roten Farbstreifen eingefasst wird. Es lenkt die Besucher über die Brücke und den Blick nach draußen, Weg- und Sichtachsen kreuzen sich hier. Die Leuchten verschwinden zwischen den Unterzügen und stören die Raumflucht des Ganges nicht. Die Fensteröffnungsmechanismen sind unauffällig, kleine Fensterflügel oben und unten, die wie ein Oberlicht geöffnet bzw. nach unten auf die

The director's office, the so-called Gropius' office, was located at the centre of the lower floor of the bridge. Here, the Bauhaus directors worked, received guests, and perhaps negotiated contracts with representatives from the industries. The Masters' and students' councils also probably convened here. The work area was designed by Gropius as a room within a room, and its structure was defined by a glass cabinet and a slightly raised ceiling. The writing desk stood at the intersection of a number of lines that defined the space, and formed a boundary within the larger space. The alcove ceiling was painted yellow and indirectly lit by tubular ceiling lights, giving the room a somewhat noble appearance.

Some of the furniture was brought by Gropius from his Weimar office, such as the cherry wood writing desk, which he designed himself, and which is available as a copy today. Other pieces of furniture were reconstructed or repainted in Dessau, such as the filing cabinets and shelves, the fitted cupboards and the display cabinet, where objects produced in the Bauhaus workshops were exhibited. These are not in situ anymore. The wall opposite the writing desk was covered with a raffia textile which was reconstructed – the same material found in the bed recesses in the studio building. All the doors in the director's room were fitted with curtains, thus absorbing sound and reducing draught. The dark brown Triolin flooring is still there, and the wall closets are still essentially original. Little more is known about the furnishing, material, colour or dimensions.

Today, few objects are as closely associated with the name of the founder of the Bauhaus as the "Gropius door handle", which was used throughout the building. It owes its fascination to its simple, geometric form of an angled square section and a cylindrical grip. The form that is seen in the Bauhaus today was designed in 1922 and was used, for instance, at the Haus Am Horn in Weimar. Up to 1930, the handles were made by the Berlin manufacturers Loevy in a number of finishes – cast brass or bronze, grey cast iron, matt or glossy, silver-plated and imitation gold-plated. In the late 1920s, other firms began to produce the handle, which in the meantime had become popular, and its form has still not been patented. Most of those in the Bauhaus Building are replicas, whereas a large number of originals have been preserved in the Masters' Houses and in the former Employment Office in Dessau. Incidentally, quite another is owed the honour of the name, as Adolf Meyer, who was a colleague in Gropius' building office in the early 20s, contributed substantially to the door handle's design.

Fensterbank geklappt werden. Während der Sanierung wurden auch die großen, zu öffnenden Flügel wiederhergestellt, die ein schnelles Durchlüften ermöglichen.

Im Zentrum des unteren Brückengeschosses befand sich das Büro des Direktors, das so genannte Gropiuszimmer. Hier haben die Direktoren des Bauhauses gearbeitet, Gäste empfangen, vielleicht Verträge mit der Industrie ausgehandelt. Wahrscheinlich tagten hier der Meisterrat und die Studierendenvertretung. Der Arbeitsbereich wurde von Gropius als Raum im Raum gestaltet, der durch eine gläserne Vitrine und eine leicht erhöhte Decke markiert war. Der Schreibtisch stand an den Schnittpunkten mehrerer den Raum definierender Linien und bildete eine Begrenzung zum großen Raum hin. Die Nischendecke wurde gelb gefasst und durch Soffitten indirekt beleuchtet, was der Raumsituation etwas Erhabenes verlieh.

Einen Teil der Möbel brachte Gropius aus seinem Weimarer Büro mit, zum Beispiel den von ihm selbst entworfenen Schreibtisch aus Kirschholz, der heute als Kopie vorhanden ist. Andere Einrichtungsteile wurden in Dessau neu gefertigt bzw. neu farbig gefasst, zum Beispiel die Aktenschränke und -regale, die Einbauschränke und vor allem die Schauvitrine, in der Produkte aus den Bauhaus-Werkstätten ausgestellt waren. Diese Möbel sind heute nicht mehr vorhanden. Die Wand gegenüber vom Schreibtisch war mit einem Bastgewebe bespannt, wie es auch im Ateliergebäude in den Bettnischen zu finden war. Vor allen Türen des Direktorenzimmers befanden sich damals Vorhänge, die den Schall schlucken und Zugluft verhindern sollten. Der dunkelbraune Triolin-Fußbodenbelag ist noch vorhanden, auch die Wandschränke sind in ihrer Substanz bauzeitlich. Darüber hinaus gibt es kaum gesicherte Fakten über die Einrichtung, über Material, Farbe und Maße.

Kaum ein anderer Gegenstand ist heute so eng mit dem Namen des Bauhaus-Gründers verknüpft wie der „Gropius-Türdrücker", der im ganzen Haus Verwendung fand. Er besticht durch seine einfache geometrische Form eines abgewinkelten Vierkantstabes und einer zylindrischen Griffrolle. Die heute bekannte Form entstand um 1922 und wurde zum Beispiel im Haus Am Horn in Weimar verwendet. Die Herstellerfirma Loevy aus Berlin lieferte bis 1930 Drücker in zahlreichen Varianten, in Messing- oder Bronzeguss, Grauguss, matt oder glänzend, versilbert und imitiert vergoldet. Ende der 1920er Jahre begannen auch andere Firmen, den inzwischen populären Drücker zu produzieren, und bis heute ist seine Form nicht geschützt. Im Bauhausgebäude existieren hauptsächlich Nachbauten, aber in den Meisterhäusern und im ehemaligen Arbeitsamt in Dessau sind sie in großer Zahl noch im Original erhalten. Im Übrigen gebührt auch einem anderen die Ehre der Namensgebung, denn Adolf Meyer, Anfang der 20er Jahre Büro-Kollege von Gropius, hat den Türdrücker maßgeblich mitgestaltet.

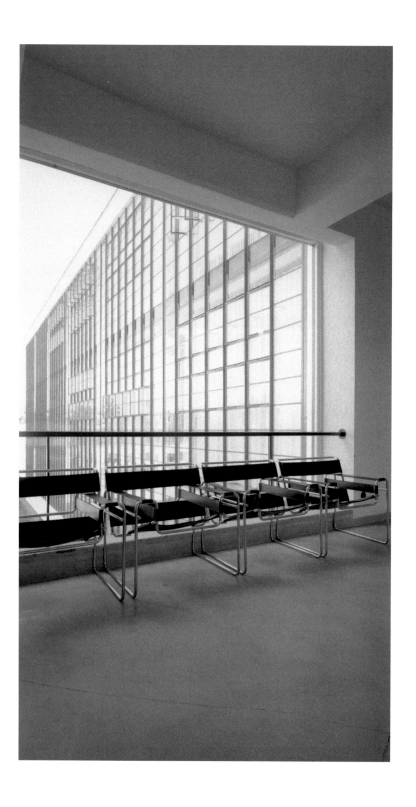

North wing The north wing, opposite the workshop tract, was reserved for the second school in the complex, the vocational school. Gropius' design was, in architectonic terms, deliberately reserved, as its main use was for traditional, theory-based teaching. More so than the studio building, staircases and bridge, however, the fascination of the north wing derives from its strong and starkly differentiated colours. The beams on each floor were painted in different colours – in blue, red and yellow, and these colours are also accordingly found in a different order on the beams and pillars in the classrooms. So e.g. on the first floor the beams on the corridor are painted yellow, in the classrooms they are painted blue.

The classrooms were separated from the central corridors by wall closets with sliding doors, which were accessible from both sides. Skylights were located above these, and the rooms at the end of the hallways had glass doors facing onto the corridors. As a whole, these features ensured a plentiful supply of daylight. The cupboards and the skylights were reconstructed during the renovation, as were the spherical lights, which lit the rooms and corridors.

As in the rest of the building, a variety of flooring materials were used in the north wing. The Triolin flooring laid in the offices was an early synthetic material, which was used for a while as a substitute for the then expensive Linoleum. The staircase steps and windowsills were made from Terrazzo. In the corridors and classrooms, magnesite flooring was used. This was a blend of screed and wood chips, which was used in housing into the 1960s due to its heat and sound insulation properties.

The north wing is also particularly interesting for visitors because of the view one has of the facing staircase and transparent corner. One has a better impression of the visual lightness of the workshop wing from here than from any other vantage point.

Nordflügel Der Nordflügel gegenüber dem Werkstättentrakt war der zweiten Schule im Gebäudekomplex vorbehalten, der Gewerblichen Berufsschule. Er wurde von Gropius architektonisch bewusst zurückhaltend gestaltet, da die Hauptfunktion der traditionelle theoretische Unterricht war. Noch mehr als das Ateliergebäude, die Treppenhäuser und die Brücke jedoch besticht der Nordflügel durch seine starke und ausdifferenzierte Farbigkeit. Die Unterzüge in jedem Geschoss wurden jeweils in einer anderen Farbe gefasst, in Blau, Rot und Gelb, und diese Farben finden sich in anderer Reihenfolge auch auf den Pfeilern der Lehrsäle wieder. So sind zum Beispiel im ersten Obergeschoss die Unterzüge im Flur gelb, in den Unterrichtsräumen blau gestrichen.

Abgetrennt waren die längs der Flure gelegenen Lehrsäle durch beidseitig nutzbare Wandschränke mit Schiebetüren. Über ihnen befanden sich Oberlichter, und die am Ende der Gänge gelegenen Räume hatten zum Flur hin Glastüren. So war insgesamt für ausreichendes Tageslicht gesorgt. Schränke und Oberlichter wurden im Zuge der Sanierung rekonstruiert, ebenso wie die Kugelleuchten, die Räume und Flure beleuchteten.

Wie im ganzen Haus wurden auch im Nordflügel unterschiedliche Fußbodenmaterialien verwendet: Das in den Büroräumen verlegte Triolin war ein früher Kunststoffbelag, der eine Zeitlang als Ersatz für das teure Linoleum fungierte. Aus Terrazzo wurden Treppenstufen und Fensterbänke gefertigt. In den Fluren sowie den Klassenräumen wurde Steinholzestrich verarbeitet, eine Mischung aus Estrich und Sägespänen, die wegen ihrer wärmeisolierenden Eigenschaften und der Trittschalldämmung bis in die 1960er Jahre im Wohnbereich Verwendung fand.

Für Besucher besonders interessant ist der Nordflügel auch wegen des Blickes, den man von hier aus auf das gegenüberliegende Treppenhaus und die transparente Ecke hat. Nirgends sonst bekommt man einen so guten Eindruck von der optischen Leichtigkeit des Werkstattflügels.

Studio building The studio building was the first hall of residence in Germany to be integrated within a University. There were 28 rooms on four storeys, 16 of which had a small balcony facing east, the other 12 facing west towards the building. Their residents could also use the communal balconies in the south, which were reached via the small kitchens at the ends of the corridors. This part of the building is still called the "Prellerhaus" in remembrance of the Weimar period. In the 19th century, the landscape painter Friedrich Preller Snr. provided a house for art students in Weimar, where many Bauhaus students later also lived. The move from the residential city of Weimar to the industrial town of Dessau was difficult for most of the students, and such reminiscence was more than welcome.

"the individual balconies turned out to be ideal places for communication, as contact to neighbours could be made from there by calling, so that one did not have to frequent one another" enthused the Bauhaus colleague Xanti Schawinsky (cit. source: Bauhaus Dessau Foundation, Margret Kentgens-Craig (Ed.), *The Bauhaus Building in Dessau* 1926 – 1999, 1998). The studio flats were incredibly popular: Over 20 m² for one person, with fitted furniture, a built-in bed, table, chairs and a washbasin too – at the time, this was pure luxury. There were showers, baths and a gym in the basement, and the roof terrace was open to all, and was used for exercise. However, only a small proportion of the approximately 140 students were able to live and work here. Most of the Bauhaus' students lived in sublet private housing in town.

The studio building is, in terms of colour, particularly intriguing. Hinnerk Scheper's idea of emphasising the form of the room with colour comes to the fore in the lobby. If one looks up through the centre of the stairwell, one can also see, as in the north wing, the differently coloured floors.

In 1930, Mies van der Rohe arranged for some of the studio flats to be combined to form classrooms, where, for example, Josef Albers taught the preliminary course and Wassily Kandinsky taught free painting. Further alterations followed, and the original fitted furniture has long disappeared. In 1989, showers were built in on each floor. Since their general renovation and refurbishment, the studio flats have been let to visitors to the Bauhaus.

Ateliergebäude Mit dem Ateliergebäude entstand das erste in eine Hochschule integrierte Studentenwohnheim in Deutschland. Auf vier Geschossen waren 28 Zimmer eingerichtet, 16 davon lagen mit einem eigenen kleinen Balkon nach Osten, die anderen zwölf nach Westen zum Gebäude hin. Deren Bewohner konnten die Gemeinschaftsbalkone im Süden benutzen, die über die Teeküchen am Ende der Gänge erreichbar waren. Der Gebäudeteil wird bis heute auch „Prellerhaus" genannt, eine Erinnerung an Weimarer Zeiten. Der Landschaftsmaler Friedrich Preller d. Ä. hatte im 19. Jahrhundert den Kunststudenten Weimars ein Wohnhaus zur Verfügung gestellt, in dem später auch viele Bauhausschüler wohnten. Der Wechsel von der Residenzstadt Weimar in die Industriestadt Dessau fiel den meisten schwer, und eine solche Reminiszenz war sehr willkommen.

„die individuellen balkone stellten sich als ideale kommunikationsstationen heraus; der kontakt mit nachbarn konnte von dort aus hergestellt werden, durch zurufe, ohne dass man sich gegenseitig aufsuchen mußte", schwärmte der Bauhäusler Xanti Schawinsky (zit. nach: Stiftung Bauhaus Dessau, Margret Kentgens-Craig (Hg.), *Das Bauhausgebäude in Dessau 1926–1999*, 1998).

Die Wohnateliers waren äußerst begehrt: Über 20 m² Wohnfläche für eine Person, dazu Einbaumöbel, eine Bettnische, Tisch und Stühle, ein Waschbecken – Luxus in dieser Zeit. Duschen, Bäder und einen Gymnastikraum gab es im Keller, und allen gemeinsam stand die Dachterrasse zur Verfügung, die ebenfalls für gymnastische Übungen genutzt wurde. Von den durchschnittlich 140 Studierenden konnte jedoch immer nur ein kleiner Teil hier leben und arbeiten, das Gros der Bauhäusler wohnte privat zur Untermiete in der Stadt.

Das Ateliergebäude ist farblich besonders interessant, denn im Vestibül wird die Idee Hinnerk Schepers deutlich, durch Farbe die Raumbildung zu unterstützen. Schaut man durch das Treppenauge nach oben, kann man auch hier, ähnlich wie im Nordflügel, die unterschiedlich farbig gefassten Geschossdecken erkennen.

1930 ließ Mies van der Rohe einige Ateliers zu Unterrichtsräumen zusammenlegen, in denen zum Beispiel Josef Albers den Vorkurs und Wassily Kandinsky seine freie Malklasse unterrichtete. Weitere Umbauten folgten, und die originalen Einbauten sind lange verschwunden. 1989 wurden in jedem Geschoss Duschen eingebaut. Nach der umfassenden Sanierung und Neuausstattung werden die Wohnateliers nun an Besucher des Bauhauses vermietet.

Workshop wing "The glass walls flowed into one another at the exact point the human eye was accustomed to finding a visible pillar. Manifested here for the first time in a large complex was the interpenetration of interior and exterior space". This citation of 1941 is by the Swiss architectural historian Sigfried Giedion. To this day, the transparent corner of the workshop wing has lost none of its original fascination.

The Bauhaus, as a home for the avant-garde in a young democracy, was to be "transparent" in the best sense, and at the same time display new materials and alternative construction methods. In the workshop wing, the reinforced concrete skeleton of the building is distinctly visible. The concrete stanchions are offset inwards, and bear the weight of the floors. The glass curtain wall has none of the static functions a brickwork wall would have had.

A small space between the curtain wall and the floors originally allowed air to circulate between all three floors – indeed, not only air, but also dust, noise, and all manner of smells from the workshops. The many radiators were placed like balustrades inside in front of the glass façade, and held users at a safe distance. As in other parts of the building, this presentation illustrated a deliberate obeisance to industry and engineering.

None of the original fittings in the workshops has been preserved, but many have been well documented. The workshops were lit by adjustable hanging lights designed by Hans Przyrembel and Marianne Brandt in 1926. Initially produced in the Bauhaus metal workshop for in-house requirements, they were later manufactured by a metals factory in Stuttgart and the Berlin-based company Fa. Schwintzer & Gräff for a variety of lighting needs. In some cases, the appearance of the aluminium shade was upgraded to increase sales: "At the time, people viewed aluminium with distaste, and we therefore sometimes sprayed the aluminium shades with paint. They were intended for general use – for the home, for restaurants and for the workshop". (Marianne Brandt, cit. *form + zweck*, 1979, No. 3). Facsimiles of the lights may now be found in their original locations in the building.

The flooring in the workshop area was either magnesite flooring, which was appropriate for industrial spaces, or non-slip riffle flooring. In keeping with the work-based character of the rooms, the reinforced masonry ceiling was not polished, but left with a visible surface texture, which was then merely lime-washed. One exception is the corner room on the first floor. This used to serve as an exhibition space, meaning that it had a representational role, and the ceilings, walls and pillars were therefore smoothly plastered.

In World War II, the curtain wall was partly demolished by a firebomb, and most of it had to be dismantled. In 1976, after a number of interim solutions, the curtain wall façade was reinstalled in its current form, albeit made from aluminium rather than steel. Since then, the glass wall has met flush with the floors, creating three separate storeys. This feature was kept during the recent renovation, as was – for reasons of monument conservation – the single glazing. Only the colour of the metal framework was altered, and this according to the recent

Werkstattflügel „Die Glaswände flossen ineinander, gerade an dem Punkt, wo das menschliche Auge gewöhnt war, einen sichtbaren Pfeiler vorzufinden. Manifestartig erschien hier zum erstenmal in einem großen Komplex die Durchdringung von Innen- und Außenraum", so formulierte es der Schweizer Architekturhistoriker Sigfried Giedion 1941. Die transparente Ecke des Werkstattflügels hat bis heute nichts von ihrer ursprünglichen Faszination verloren. Das Bauhaus sollte als Ort der Avantgarde in einer jungen Demokratie im besten Sinne „durchschaubar" sein und zugleich neue Materialien und Konstruktionsmöglichkeiten zeigen. Im Werkstattflügel ist das Stahlbetonskelett des Bauhauses deutlich zu erkennen. Die Betonpfeiler sind nach innen versetzt und tragen das Gewicht der Geschossdecken. Die Glasvorhangfassade hat keine statische Funktion mehr, wie es eine gemauerte Wand gehabt hätte. Ein kleiner Abstand zwischen Vorhangfassade und Fußbodenebenen ließ ursprünglich die Luft zwischen allen drei Geschossen zirkulieren. Allerdings nicht nur die Luft, sondern auch Staub, Lärm und allerlei Gerüche aus den verschiedenen Werkstätten. Die zahlreichen Heizkörper wurden wie Brüstungen innen vor die Glasfassade gesetzt und hielten die Nutzer auf Abstand. Wie in anderen Teilen des Gebäudes war diese Präsentation eine gewollte Verbeugung vor Industrie und Technik.

Von den Werkstatteinrichtungen ist nichts erhalten geblieben, aber vieles gut dokumentiert. Beleuchtet wurden die Werkstatträume durch die von Hans Przyrembel und Marianne Brandt 1926 entworfenen Zugpendelleuchten. Zunächst in der Metallwerkstatt des Bauhauses für den Eigenbedarf produziert, wurden sie danach von einem Stuttgarter Metallwerk sowie der Fa. Schwintzer & Gräff in Berlin für unterschiedliche Beleuchtungszwecke hergestellt. Der aus Aluminium bestehende Schirm wurde in manchen Fällen aufgewertet, um ihn besser verkaufen zu können: „Den Leuten war Aluminium damals etwas Fatales, wir haben die Schirme deshalb manchmal auch farbgespritzt. Sie war für alles gedacht, für die Wohnstube, für Gaststätten, für die Werkstatt." (Marianne Brandt, zit. nach: *form + zweck*, 1979) Die originalgetreu rekonstruierten Zugpendelleuchten befinden sich nun wieder an ihren ursprünglichen Orten im Haus.

Als Fußbodenbeläge wurden in den Werkstätten Steinholzestrich (Magnesitestrich), der für Industriehallen geeignet war, oder rutschsicherer Riffelestrich verwendet. Dem Arbeitscharakter der Räume entsprechend wurden die Steineisendecken nicht verputzt, sondern in ihrer Struktur sichtbar gelassen und nur weiß geschlämmt. Eine Ausnahme ist der Eckraum im Erdgeschoss, der früher als Ausstellungsraum fungierte, also einen repräsentativen Zweck erfüllte und dessen Decke, Wände sowie Stützen glatt verputzt wurden.

Im Zweiten Weltkrieg wurde die Stahlkonstruktion durch eine Brandbombe teilweise zerstört und musste fast komplett abgenommen werden. Nach verschiedenen Zwischenlösungen wurde die Vorhangfassade 1976 in ihrer jetzigen Form installiert – aus Aluminium, nicht aus Stahl. Die Glaswand schließt seitdem mit den Fußbodenebenen ab, sodass drei separate Geschosse entstanden. Dieser Zustand wurde auch bei der jüngsten Sanierung belassen, ebenso wie es aus denkmalpflegerischen Gründen nach wie vor nur eine Einfachverglasung gibt. Verändert wurde nach neuestem restauratorischen Befund lediglich die Farbe der Metallkonstruktionen. Die Fensterrahmen am Bauhaus waren nicht schwarz, wie stets angenommen, sondern außen anthrazitgrau und innen hellgrau, fast weiß. Dadurch wirkt das Bauhausgebäude heute innen lichter und außen eleganter als noch vor wenigen Jahren. Die Kontraste verstärkende Schwarzweißfotografie der 1920er Jahre hat hier Architekten, Kunsthistoriker und Restauratoren lange Zeit in die Irre geführt.

Die starke Farbigkeit des Bauhauses zeigt sich in allen Teilen des Gebäudes, so auch im Südtreppenhaus, das die Werkstätten separat erschloss. Die Restauratoren legten hier ein kräftiges Rot frei, das durch seine Pigmentierung eine bemerkenswerte Tiefe erreicht und mit weißen und grauen Wandflächen kombiniert wurde. Mit den rekonstruierten zylindrischen Leuchten von Marianne Brandt sowie der vertikalen, sich über vier Geschosse erstreckenden Leuchtenkonstruktion von Max Krajewski befindet sich hier an etwas abgelegener Stelle ein ästhetisches Kleinod.

findings of restoration research. The window frames at the Bauhaus were not black, as was invariable assumed, but anthracite grey on the outside and light grey (almost white) on the inside. The Bauhaus Building therefore seems lighter on the inside and more elegant from the outside than it did just a few years ago. In this case, architects, art historians and restorers were long misled by the contrast-enhancing black and white photography of the 1920s.

The Bauhaus' intense use of colour is now visible in all parts of the building, including the southern staircase, which provided a separate access into the workshops. Here, restorers exposed a strong red colour, which has a remarkable intensity thanks to its pigmentation, and which was combined with white and grey wall surfaces. With the replicated cylindrical lights by Marianne Brandt and the vertical lighting system by Max Krajewski, which extends to all four floors, this somewhat secluded space is an aesthetic treasure.

Ausbildung

Education and training

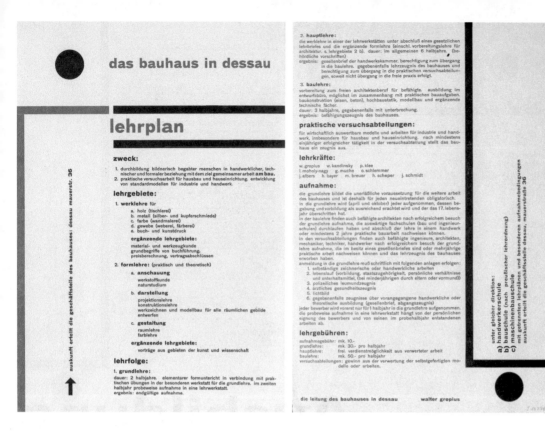

Lehrplan des Bauhaus Dessau,
Vorder- und Rückansicht, 1925
Bauhaus Dessau curriculum,
front and back view, 1925

„Die Bauhauswerkstätten sind im wesentlichen Laboratorien, in denen vervielfältigungsreife, für die heutige Zeit typische Geräte sorgfältig im Modell entwickelt und dauernd verbessert werden. Das Bauhaus will in diesen Laboratorien einen neuen, nicht vorhandenen Typ von Mitarbeiter für Industrie und Handwerk heranbilden, der Technik und Form in gleichem Maße beherrscht." (Walter Gropius, in: *Bauhaus Dessau – Grundsätze der Bauhaus-Produktion*, 1926)

Die Ausbildung am Bauhaus war ein praktisch orientiertes Studium, das im Idealfall aus dem Vorkurs, einer Werkstattlehre mit Gesellenbrief und einem Architekturstudium bestand. In den meisten Fällen jedoch blieb dieser Studienaufbau Theorie. In der Weimarer Zeit absolvierte immerhin eine Vielzahl von Schülern den Vorkurs, eine dreijährige Lehre und die Gesellenprüfung vor den regionalen Handwerkskammern. Viele der rund 1.250 Studierenden, die zwischen 1919 und 1933 am Bauhaus eingeschrieben waren, blieben jedoch nur ein oder zwei Semester, einfach, um sich vom Ort und den interessanten Künstlerpersönlichkeiten sowie der kreativen Atmosphäre inspirieren zu lassen.

Im obligatorischen Vorkurs wurden zunächst vor allem die kreativen Fähigkeiten der Erstsemester getestet – es war ein Probekurs, in dem viel experimentiert wurde. Gleichzeitig ergab sich so die Möglichkeit, die Besten auszusuchen und den hohen Qualitätsstandard der Schule zu sichern.

"The Bauhaus workshops are, in essence, laboratories, where typical tools of the modern age suitable for mass production are painstakingly designed in model form and continuously improved upon. The Bauhaus aims to educate a new, as yet non-existent type of worker for the industries and trades, who has an equal command of both engineering and form". (Walter Gropius, in: *Bauhaus Dessau – Grundsätze der Bauhaus-Produktion*, 1926).

Education at the Bauhaus was a practice-based course of study, which ideally consisted of a preliminary course, a workshop apprenticeship and a course of studies in architecture. However, in most cases, this educational structure remained theoretical. In the Weimar period, a number of students nevertheless completed a preliminary course, a three-year apprenticeship and absolved the examinations of the regional chamber of trade. However, many of the approximately 1,250 students who enrolled at the Bauhaus between 1919 and 1933 stayed just one or two terms, simply to be inspired by the place, the fascinating artistic personalities and the creative atmosphere.

In the obligatory preliminary course, the creative abilities of the new students were first put to the test; this was a trial course, where the focus was on experimentation. This also made it possible to select the best students, and thus safeguard the school's high standards.

The organisation of the workshops, particularly in the Weimar period, was unusual, as there were two Masters per workshop:

Die Organisation der Werkstätten war vor allem in der Weimarer Zeit eine Besonderheit, denn es gab jeweils zwei Meister pro Werkstatt: die Werk-Meister für die handwerklich-technische sowie die Form-Meister für die künstlerische Ausbildung. In dieser Position arbeiteten die Maler, die dem Bauhaus schnell zu dessen gutem Ruf verhalfen, wie zum Beispiel Lyonel Feininger, Oskar Schlemmer oder Wassily Kandinsky. Mit dem Umzug nach Dessau änderte sich dieses Ausbildungssystem. Als Werkstattleiter wurden die so genannten Jungmeister eingesetzt, Bauhausstudenten, die am Staatlichen Bauhaus Weimar gelernt hatten und nun ihre Fähigkeiten an die nächste Generation weitergeben sollten. Zu ihnen gehörten z.B. Marcel Breuer in der Tischlerei, Herbert Bayer in der Druck- und Reklamewerkstatt und Gunta Stölzl in der Weberei.

the Technical Master, who taught the trades and engineering and the Form Master, who provided the arts-based education. These positions were held by the painters and these, such as Lyonel Feininger, Oskar Schlemmer and Wassily Kandinsky, quickly established the Bauhaus' good reputation. With the relocation to Dessau, this educational system changed. So-called Junior Masters were put in charge of the workshops – Bauhaus students who had studied at the Staatliches Bauhaus Weimar, and who were now to pass on their skills to the next generation. These included, for example, Marcel Breuer in the carpentry workshop, Herbert Bayer in the printing and advertising workshop, and Gunta Stölzl in the textile workshop.

Die erste Riege der Meister, die Gropius nach Weimar berief, war eine reine Männergarde: Paul Klee, Wassily Kandinsky, Oskar Schlemmer, Gerhard Marcks, Johannes Itten, Lyonel Feininger. Frauen gelangten im Kaiserreich und kurz danach kaum in solche Lehrpositionen. Auch Gropius selbst sah in weiblichen Studierenden weniger Künstlerinnen als Kunstgewerblerinnen, wie sie etwas abfällig genannt wurden. Nach Gründung der Weimarer Republik hatten Frauen in Deutschland erstmals ungehinderten Zugang zu Kunsthochschulen, und ihr Anteil betrug 1919 über 50 Prozent der Bauhausstudierenden. Es hieß schnell: „Keine unnötigen Experimente!", denn Gropius wollte eine Eliteschule, kein Kunstgewerbe. Höchstens ein Drittel der Studierenden sollte zukünftig weiblich sein. Dennoch setzten sich immer wieder einzelne Talente über die inhaltlichen Beschränkungen hinweg. Marianne Brandt in der Metallwerkstatt, Margaret Leiteritz in der Wandmalerei oder Vera Meyer-Waldeck in der Tischlerei sind nur einige Beispiele, und auch manche Weberin brachte es zu Weltruhm, wie Anni Albers. Am Ende blieb die Bilanz für die Studentinnen auf jeden Fall positiv, denn das Bauhaus trug mit seiner qualitativ hochwertigen Ausbildung, seinem international hervorragenden Ruf und seinen guten Kontakten zur Industrie erheblich zur Professionalisierung all seiner Studierenden bei. Aus dem Schatten der Meister konnten allerdings nur wenige heraustreten, egal ob männlich oder weiblich.

The first team of Masters that Gropius appointed in Weimar was an all-male brigade: Paul Klee, Wassily Kandinsky, Oskar Schlemmer, Gerhard Marcks, Johannes Itten and Lyonel Feininger. Women seldom acquired such teaching positions in the German empire or shortly afterwards. Even Gropius saw female students less as artists than as applied artists – a somewhat disparaging term. After the foundation of the Weimar Republic, women in Germany had unrestricted access to art schools for the first time, and in 1919, they made up over 50 percent of the students. As Gropius wanted an elite school, rather than an arts and crafts school, it was soon a case of "no unnecessary experiments!" In future, only a third of the students were to be female. Nevertheless, individual talents were often able to surmount these restrictions. Marianne Brandt in the metal workshop, Margaret Leiteritz in the wall painting workshop and Vera Meyer-Waldeck in the carpentry are just a few examples, and a number of weavers, such as Anni Albers, became world famous. Ultimately, the balance was most certainly in the students' favour as the Bauhaus' high educational standards, excellent reputation worldwide and good contacts to industry contributed significantly to the professionalisation of all its students. Nevertheless, only a few students were able to emerge from the shadows cast by their Masters, whether male of female.

Konrad Püschel, Grätenfaltung, Material-übung aus dem Vorkurs bei Josef Albers, 1926/27
Konrad Püschel, zigzag folding technique, exercise from Josef Albers' preliminary course, 1926/27

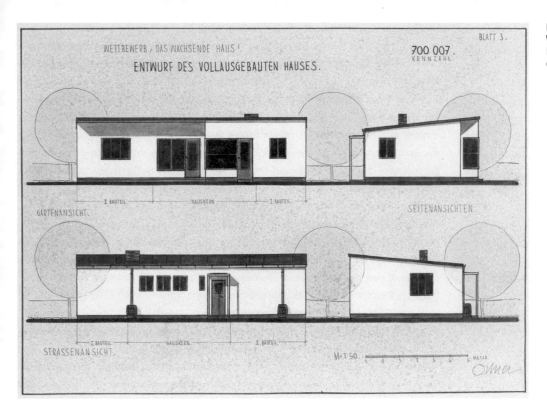

Rudolf Ortner, Das wachsende Haus,
Wettbewerbsentwurf (Blatt 3), 1931/32
Rudolf Ortner, "The Growing House",
competition draft (page 3), 1931/32

Bauabteilung Erst 1927 wurde am Bauhaus eine Architekturklasse eingerichtet; bis dahin konnten interessierte Studierende nur in Gropius' privatem Bauatelier mitarbeiten und lernen. Ihren Platz bekam die Abteilung im oberen Brückengeschoss. Das große Büro war zum Gang hin mit einem langen Einbauschrank versehen und durch Glastüren von den anderen Gebäudeflügeln getrennt.

Als ersten Leiter der Bauabteilung berief Gropius den Schweizer Architekten Hannes Meyer, der sich durch seinen Entwurf für den Völkerbundpalast in Genf einen Namen gemacht hatte. Auf Meyer wirkte das Bauhaus zu dieser Zeit „sektenhaft und ästhetisch", auch als er 1928 Direktor der Institution wurde: „Inzüchtige Theorien versperrten jeden Zugang zur lebensrichtigen Gestaltung: Der Würfel war Trumpf, und seine Seiten waren gelb, rot, blau, weiß, grau, schwarz. Diesen Bauhauswürfel gab man dem Kind zum Spiel und dem Bauhaus-Snob zur Spielerei. Das Quadrat war rot. Der Kreis war blau. Das Dreieck war gelb. Man saß und schlief auf der farbigen Geometrie der Möbel. Man bewohnte die gefärbten Plastiken der Häuser. Auf deren Fußböden lagen als Teppiche die seelischen Komplexe junger Mädchen. Überall erdrosselte die Kunst das Leben. So entstand eine tragikomische Situation: Als Bauhausleiter bekämpfte ich den Bauhausstil." (Hannes Meyer, *Mein Hinauswurf aus dem Bauhaus*, Offener Brief an Oberbürgermeister Hesse, Dessau, 1930) Meyers Anliegen war das „funktionell-kollektivistisch-konstruktive Bauen", das sich an wissenschaftlichen Erkenntnissen und täglichen Erfordernissen ausrichten sollte. Meyer stellte in der Architektur soziale Anliegen bewusst stärker in den Vordergrund als Gropius.

Da es an öffentlichen Aufträgen mangelte, wurde zunächst vor allem die Theorie gelehrt. Besonders unter Ludwig Hilberseimer, der ab 1929 am Bauhaus unter anderem Städtebau unterrichtete, wurde die Stadtplanung systematisch analysiert, und Meyer holte zahlreiche in- und ausländische Fachleute für Vorträge nach Dessau.

Department of architecture A department of architecture was first established at the Bauhaus in 1927. Before that, interested students were only able to work and learn in Gropius' private architectural office. The department was located on the upper floor of the bridge. The large office was furnished with a long built-in cupboard on the corridor side, and separated from the other wings of the building by glass doors. Gropius appointed the Swiss architect Hannes Meyer, who had made a name for himself with his design for the League of Nations building (Völkerbundpalast) in Geneva, as the first head of the department of architecture. At the time, Meyer found the Bauhaus "sectarian and aesthetic" – even when he became the institute's director in 1928: "Crude theories obstructed every approach to design appropriate for living: The cube was the trump, and its sides were yellow, red, blue, white, grey and black. This Bauhaus cube was given to the child to play with, and to the Bauhaus snob as child's play. The square was red. The circle was blue. The triangle was yellow. One sat and slept on the coloured geometry of the furniture. One inhabited the coloured sculptures of the houses. On their floors lay, as carpeting, the emotional complexes of young girls. Everywhere, art throttled life. Thus arose a tragicomic situation: As the director of the Bauhaus, I battled the Bauhaus style". (Hannes Meyer, *My expulsion from the Bauhaus*, open letter to Lord Mayor Hesse, Dessau, 1930). Meyer's cause was "functional-collective-constructive building", which was to cater to scientific knowledge and the necessities of daily life. In architecture, Meyer deliberately prioritized social concerns to a far greater extent than Gropius.

Since there was a shortage of public commissions, teaching initially focused on theory. Particularly under Ludwig Hilberseimer, who from 1929 taught (among other things) urban development, town planning was systematically analysed, and Meyer summoned numerous national and international experts to Dessau for lectures.

Practical work was nevertheless also possible. The five Balcony Access Houses in south Dessau were designed, and their construction supervised, by Hannes Meyer and the students. The Bundesschule des Allgemeinen Deutschen Gewerkschaftsbundes (ADGB) in Bernau near Berlin, which was designed by Hannes Meyer and Hans Wittwer, became a successful testing ground for the students, and brought the Bauhaus good reviews.

In 1930 under Ludwig Mies van der Rohe, the department of architecture grew in an entirely new direction. Spatial harmonies, proportions, fine materials – architecture moved into the heart of the education system. Now, during the Great Depression, commissions were rarer than ever. Mies altered the educational structure, and students were now able to enrol in the department of architecture without completing the preceding apprenticeship. The Bauhaus became a school of architecture – a departure from Gropius' original concept of a broadly educated craftsman-artist-architect.

Aber es konnte auch praktisch gearbeitet werden. Die fünf Laubenganghäuser in Dessau-Süd wurden gemeinsam von den Studierenden und Hannes Meyer entworfen und baulich betreut. Auch die Bundesschule des Allgemeinen Deutschen Gewerkschaftsbundes (ADGB) in Bernau bei Berlin, die Hannes Meyer und Hans Wittwer entwarfen, wurde zum gelungenen Übungsfeld für die Studierenden und brachte dem Bauhaus gute Kritiken ein.

Mit Ludwig Mies van der Rohe erhielt die Bauabteilung 1930 eine völlig andere Ausrichtung. Raumharmonien, Proportionen, edle Materialien – die Baukunst rückte in den Mittelpunkt der Ausbildung. Aufträge waren nun, während der Weltwirtschaftskrise, noch spärlicher. Mies änderte die Ausbildungsstruktur, und Studierende konnten sich nun auch ohne vorherige Lehre für die Architekturklasse einschreiben. Das Bauhaus wurde zu einer Architekturschule, die nur noch wenig mit der Gropius'schen Ursprungsidee des universell gebildeten Handwerker-Künstler-Architekten zu tun hatte.

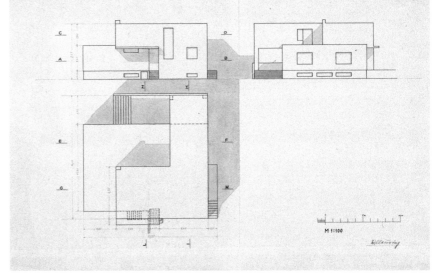

Hugo Clausing, Meisterhäuser Dessau, Direktorenhaus, Ansichten mit eingezeichnetem Schattenwurf der Morgensonne. Übung aus dem Unterricht in darstellender Geometrie bei Friedrich Köhn, 1928
Hugo Clausing, Dessau Masters' Houses, Directors' House, perspectives showing shadows created by the morning sun. Exercise from a class in illustrative geometry by Friedrich Köhn, 1928

Bühnenwerkstatt Keine andere Kunst- und Architekturschule in Deutschland hatte zu Beginn der 1920er Jahre eine Bühnenabteilung. Nur die Berliner Künstlergruppe „Der Sturm" führte zuvor bereits eine Theaterklasse im Lehrplan. Das Bauhaus wollte auch auf diesem Gebiet die Künste zusammenführen, und die Bühne verstand sich als experimenteller Raum für die Suche nach dem Gesamtkunstwerk.

In Weimar leitete Lothar Schreyer ab 1921 die Bühne, aber sein mystisch-religiöses Spiel war bald unzeitgemäß und wurde von den Schülern nicht unterstützt. 1923 übernahm der Maler und Bildhauer Oskar Schlemmer die Theaterwerkstatt. Sein bereits zuvor choreografiertes Triadisches Ballett, ein abstraktes Theater für drei Tänzer in drei Akten, war zwar in Stuttgart ein großer Erfolg, stieß bei weiteren Aufführungen jedoch auf Unverständnis. Die Zeit war noch nicht reif für ein handlungsfreies Tanztheater, das vornehmlich die Bewegung im Raum zum Thema hatte, und auch die kubistisch anmutenden Kostüme lösten oft Befremden aus.

In Dessau entwickelten Oskar Schlemmer und seine Studierenden weitere experimentelle Raumtänze: Formen- und Gestentanz, Raum- und Reifentanz, Stäbe- und Scheibentanz, bei denen Raum, Bewegung, Form und Farbe miteinander in Beziehung gesetzt wurden. Andor Weininger und Xanti Schawinski, Lou Scheper und Joost Schmidt waren Schlemmers wichtigste Mitstreiter.

Weininger rief 1924 auch die Bauhaus-Kapelle ins Leben, die zunächst in unterschiedlicher Besetzung improvisierte, meist mit Banjo und Klarinette, Saxophon, Schlagzeug und Klavier. Nach 1928 wurde die Band professioneller und galt bald als eine der besten Jazzkapellen in der Nähe Berlins.

Theatre workshop In the early 1920s, no other school for art and architecture in Germany had a theatre department. Only the Berlin art group "Der Sturm" had previously included a theatre class in their curriculum. The Bauhaus wanted to unite the arts in this field too, and the theatre was seen as an experimental space serving the quest for the Gesamtkunstwerk.

From 1921 in Weimar, the theatre was directed by Lothar Schreyer, but his mystic/religious ventures were soon outmoded, and lost the support of the students. In 1923, the theatre workshop was taken over by the painter and sculptor Oskar Schlemmer. Although his previously choreographed triadic ballet, an abstract piece for three dancers in three acts was a great success in Stuttgart, it met with a lack of understanding at subsequent performances. The time was not ripe for plot-free dance theatre where the main subject was movement in space, and the cubist-influenced costumes often provoked a sense of alienation.

In Dessau, Oskar Schlemmer and his students developed other experimental dances, such as the form and gesture dance, the space and hoop dance and the stick and disc dance, where space, movement, form and colour were examined in relation to one another. Andor Weininger, Xanti Schawinski, Lou Scheper and Joost Schmidt were Schlemmer's most important comrades in arms.

In 1924, Weininger also brought the Bauhaus band to life. This initially improvised with a varied cast, usually incorporating banjo, clarinet, saxophone, drums and piano. The band became increasingly professional from 1928 on, and was soon accepted as one of the best jazz bands in the Berlin area.

Gestentanz III, Szenenaufnahme mit Oskar Schlemmer, Werner Siedhoff und Walter Kaminsky, 1927
Gesture dance III, photo of a scene with Oskar Schlemmer, Werner Siedhoff and Walter Kaminsky, 1927

László Moholy-Nagy, Prospekt
für die Bauhausbücher, 1928
László Moholy-Nagy, brochure
for the Bauhaus books, 1928

Printing and advertising workshop

In 1926, the printing workshop was located in the basement of the workshop wing, alongside a caretaker's flat. The workshop was equipped with new machines, and had its own composing room. The school's commercial papers, leaflets, brochures, placards and forms could be printed here independently. Only one simple and unadorned font was used: the Akzidenz Grotesk. This was available in all type sizes, in various sets, and as wooden printing blocks. The head of the workshop in Dessau, as Junior Master, was Herbert Bayer, and by now commissions were accepted from trade and industry. In general, work was defined less by a systematic educational process than by "learning by doing". While László Moholy-Nagy had already proclaimed the "New Typography" in 1923, under Bayer a kind of "corporate design" of the Bauhaus finally came into being. Shades of red, and black, became the predominant printing colours. Bars, circles, lines and even photographs became graphic elements. The introduction of the German industrial norms for all things related to print streamlined production, and between 1925 and 1928, the use of lower case letters in Bauhaus publications prevailed. The prominent exception was the lettering on the building itself, for which Herbert Bayer designed capital letters.

In 1928, Joost Schmidt became head of the now re-named advertising workshop. In addition to purely typographical work, the department was also heavily involved in exhibition design. Training in photography was first included in the course of studies a year later. The products made in the Bauhaus workshop for printing and advertising still influence the way we understand modern typography today.

Druck- und Reklamewerkstatt

Im Sockelgeschoss des Werkstattflügels befand sich 1926 neben einer Hausmeisterwohnung auch die Druckwerkstatt – neu mit Maschinen ausgestattet und mit eigener Setzerei. Geschäftspapiere, Prospekte, Plakate und Formulare der Schule konnten hier selbst hergestellt werden. Verwendet wurde eine einzige schlichte, schnörkellose Schrift, die Akzidenz Grotesk. Sie war in allen Schriftgraden und verschiedenen Garnituren vorhanden, auch als Plakatbuchstaben aus Holz. Werkstattleiter in Dessau war als Jungmeister Herbert Bayer, und nun wurden auch Aufträge aus Industrie und Handel angenommen. Insgesamt bestimmte weniger eine systematische Ausbildung als vielmehr „learning by doing" die Arbeit.

Schon 1923 hatte László Moholy-Nagy eine „Neue Typografie" proklamiert, unter Bayer entstand schließlich so etwas wie das „Corporate Design" des Bauhauses. Rot-Töne und Schwarz waren die dominierenden Druckfarben. Balken, Kreise, Linien und sogar Fotografien wurden zu grafischen Elementen. Die Einführung der Deutschen Industrie-Normen für Drucksachen vereinheitlichte die Produktion, und zwischen 1925 und 1928 setzte sich in Bauhauspublikationen die Kleinschreibung durch. Prominente Ausnahme war der Schriftzug am Bauhausgebäude selbst, für den Herbert Bayer Großbuchstaben entwarf.

1928 wurde Joost Schmidt Leiter der Reklameabteilung, wie sie nun hieß. Neben rein typografischer Arbeit wurden hier vor allem Ausstellungen gestaltet. Ein Jahr später erst wurde die fotografische Ausbildung in den Lehrkanon aufgenommen. Die Produkte der Werkstatt für Druck und Reklame des Bauhauses sind bis heute prägend für das, was wir unter moderner Typografie verstehen.

Foto- und Filmabteilung Fotografie und Film spielten in der Bauhaus-Ausbildung erst sehr spät eine Rolle. Es waren eher einzelne Künstlerinnen und Künstler wie László Moholy-Nagy, Marianne Brandt, Walter Peterhans oder Lucia Moholy, die diese Disziplinen am Bauhaus populär machten. Jeder zweite Studierende am Bauhaus fotografierte – mit oder ohne Ausbildung.

In den 1920er Jahren wurden die Kameras einfacher und preiswerter und die Fotografie zum verbreiteten Medium. Der fantasievolle Blick durch den Sucher kreierte ein „Neues Sehen", das ungewohnte Blickwinkel festhielt. Vogel- und Froschperspektive, das Spiel mit Licht und Schatten bekamen künstlerischen Stellenwert und wurden bewusst zur Verfremdung alltäglicher Gegenstände oder Szenerien eingesetzt. Überblendungen, Montagen und Collagen erweiterten das Spektrum.

Besonders die osteuropäischen Konstruktivisten, zu denen auch Moholy-Nagy zählte, waren auf diesem Gebiet führend. Er fertigte Fotogramme, führte Filmexperimente durch und machte viele Bauhausstudierende überhaupt erst mit dem „Lichtbildnern" vertraut. Für Walter Gropius hingegen blieb die Fotografie eher Mittel zum Zweck, zum Beispiel zur Dokumentation der Bauhausbauten und -objekte. Erst 1929 wurde unter Hannes Meyer eine Abteilung für Fotografie eingerichtet. Zugeordnet war sie zunächst der Werkstatt für Druck und Reklame, bevor sie 1930 unter Walter Peterhans ein eigenes Fach wurde.

Photography and film department Photography and film did not play a role in education at the Bauhaus until much later on. These disciplines became popular at the Bauhaus thanks to individual artists such as László Moholy-Nagy, Marianne Brandt, Walter Peterhans and Lucia Moholy. Every second student at the Bauhaus took photographs, whether trained or not.

In the 1920s, cameras became simpler and less expensive, and photography became a common medium. The imaginative potential of the view through the viewfinder created a "New Vision" that captured unusual vantage points. Aerial and ground level perspectives and the interplay of light and shadow gained artistic value, and were deliberately used to distort everyday objects or scenarios. Cross fading, montage and collage enhanced the spectrum.

The Eastern European constructivists, who included Moholy-Nagy, were leaders in this field. Moholy-Nagy produced photograms, experimented with the medium of film, and introduced the camera to many of the students at the Bauhaus for the very first time. For Gropius, however, photography remained a means to an end, i.e., for the documentation of the Bauhaus buildings and artefacts. A department of photography was first set up in 1929 under Hannes Meyer. It was initially part of the workshop for printing and advertising, and then became an independent department in 1930 under Walter Peterhans.

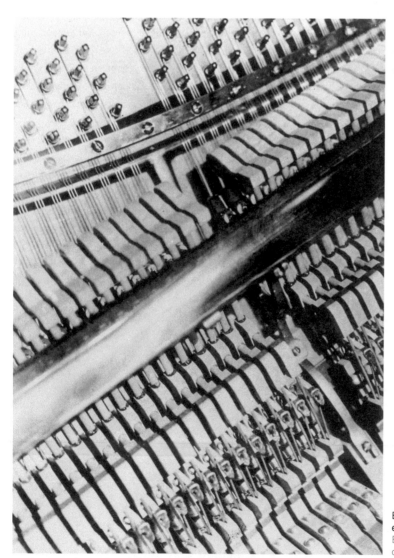

Edmund Collein, Das Innere eines Konzertflügels, 1928
Edmund Collein, "The interior of a grand piano", 1928

Eugen Batz, Gewinkelt. Aus der
Malklasse bei Paul Klee, 1930
Eugen Batz, "Gewinkelt", from a
painting class given by Paul Klee,
1930

Painting classes For Walter Gropius, particularly in the early years, painting was an important part of the interdisciplinary curriculum. The creative points of departure were colour and form, and these were an important part of the preliminary course. Studies were not limited to life drawing, portrait painting and colour theory, but also included the analysis of line and plane, light and shade, and surface and material. The elementary principles taught here formed the foundations for design at the Bauhaus for many years. László Moholy-Nagy, Oskar Schlemmer and Josef Albers in particular were able to put their artistic approach into practice in the workshops.

Most of the painters, such as Kandinsky, Feininger and Klee, stayed true to the traditional concept of painting, and their importance to education at the Bauhaus became increasingly controversial. In 1929, free painting classes were set up under Hannes Meyer. While this represented a revaluation of painting, it also challenged the prevailing interdisciplinary concept of education at the Bauhaus. This anti-traditionalist view was shared by Mies van der Rohe, who, in 1930, greatly reduced the importance of painting at the Bauhaus.

Malklassen Die Malerei hatte für Walter Gropius gerade in den ersten Jahren einen hohen Stellenwert innerhalb des interdisziplinären Lehrkanons. Farbe und Form waren der kreative Ausgangspunkt und ein wichtiger Teil des Vorkurses. Nicht nur Aktzeichnen, Porträtmalerei und Farbenlehre standen auf dem Programm, auch analytische Studien von Linie und Fläche, Hell und Dunkel, Oberfläche und Material wurden betrieben. Die hier gelehrten elementaren Prinzipien bildeten viele Jahre die Grundlage für die Gestaltung am Bauhaus. Besonders László Moholy-Nagy, Oskar Schlemmer und Josef Albers konnten ihre künstlerische Auffassung auch in ihrer praktischen Werkstattarbeit umsetzen.

Die meisten Maler wie Kandinsky, Feininger und Klee blieben dem traditionellen Tafelbild verhaftet, und ihre Bedeutung innerhalb der Bauhaus-Ausbildung war zunehmend umstritten. 1929 wurden unter Hannes Meyer Freie Malklassen eingerichtet. Einerseits war dies eine Aufwertung der Malerei, andererseits wurde damit der bisherige interdisziplinäre Bauhaus-Unterricht in Frage gestellt. Ähnlich sah es ab 1930 Ludwig Mies van der Rohe, der die Bedeutung der Malerei stark einschränkte.

Marianne Brandt, Sahnegießer,
Zuckerschale und Tablett, Silber, 1928
Marianne Brandt, cream jug, sugar bowl
and tray, silver, 1928

Marianne Brandt, Hin Bredendieck, Kandem-
Schreibtischleuchte Nr. 679 dgr., 1928/29
Marianne Brandt, Hin Bredendieck, "Kandem"
desk lamp no. 679, 1928/29

Metallwerkstatt In Weimar war die Metallwerkstatt zunächst eine reine Gold- und Silberschmiede, und es wurden vor allem einzelne Kannen, Kerzenleuchter und Dosen in Handarbeit gefertigt. Mit der Übernahme der Werkstatt durch László Moholy-Nagy, den „Künstler-Ingenieur," begannen die Studierenden 1923, sich mit neuen Materialien zu befassen und Geschirr und Lampen zu entwerfen. Die Grundformen Kreis, Kugel und Zylinder waren Ausgangspunkt vieler Entwürfe. Auch die Bauhaus-Leuchte von Wilhelm Wagenfeld und Carl Jakob Jucker entstand noch in Weimar, und schon 1924 standen über vierzig Objekte zur industriellen Vervielfältigung bereit.

In Dessau wurde die Metallwerkstatt im zweiten Obergeschoss des Werkstattflügels mit Hilfe der Junkers-Werke besser ausgestattet und fand zunehmend Kooperationspartner in der Industrie. Gemeinsam mit Firmen wie Kandem in Leipzig oder Schwintzer & Gräff in Berlin entstanden zahlreiche Entwürfe, die inzwischen zu den Klassikern modernen Designs gehören. Nachdem Moholy-Nagy 1928 das Bauhaus verlassen hatte, übernahm Marianne Brandt als herausragende Metall- und Leuchtendesignerin die Werkstatt, bis diese in die Ausbauwerkstatt integriert wurde. Heute sind viele von Brandts Entwürfen bzw. die ihrer Kollegen wieder an ihren ursprünglichen Orten im Bauhausgebäude zu sehen.

Metal workshop In Weimar, the metal workshop was initially just a gold and silversmith's, and produced mainly one-off hand-worked cans, candlesticks and tins. In 1923, when the workshop was taken over by the "artist engineer" László Moholy-Nagy, the students began to work with new materials and to design tableware and lamps. Many designs were based on the basic forms of circles, spheres and cylinders. Wilhelm Wagenfeld and Carl Jakob Jucker's "Bauhaus lamp" was also designed in the Weimar period, and by 1924, more than forty objects were ready for industrial reproduction.

In Dessau, the metal workshop on the second floor of the workshop wing was newly equipped with the assistance of the Junkers factory, and it accumulated cooperation partners from the industries. In collaboration with companies such as Kandem in Leipzig or Schwinzer & Gräff in Berlin, numerous products came into being, which have meanwhile become modern design classics. After Moholy-Nagy's departure from the Bauhaus in 1928, Marianne Brandt, who was its most prolific metal and lighting designer, took over the workshop until this was integrated into the construction workshop. Many of Brandt's designs and those of her associates may now be seen once more in their original locations in the Bauhaus Building.

Textile workshop "Where there is wool, there is also a woman weaving, even if only to pass the time", mocked Oskar Schlemmer: At the time, the textile workshop in Weimar still held the traditional view of applied arts and crafts as "woman's work". The young women knotted, embroidered, sewed and weaved, although they had to teach themselves most of the technical aspects of weaving. Tapestries with narrative motifs and abstract experiments in weaving came into being. The textile workshop was always one of the largest Bauhaus workshops, not least because most of the women were sent there.

In Dessau, the painter Georg Muche was the Form Master, but in 1927, Gunta Stölzl went on to become the Bauhaus' first female Junior Master. The profile of the workshop, which was located on the first floor, changed, and the modernised department now developed prototypes, usually of utility materials, for industry. Experiments with new fibres such as cellophane led to the development of materials with innovative properties, i.e., materials affording sound insulation, which reflected light, or which were particularly durable.

The advent of tubular steel furniture brought the need for new upholstery materials, as the lack of padding meant that the traditional horsehair and cotton materials were subject to an increased strain, which they were incapable of withstanding. In the late 1920s, the Bauhaus weavers therefore developed a unique, extremely durable material, the so-called Eisengarngewebe (literally, iron yarn). In 1928, customers could select a black, rust-coloured or grey upholstery material from a marketing catalogue issued by Breuer-Möbel. By the 1930s, Eisengarn had become a standard upholstery material.

In 1932, the interior designer Lilly Reich took over the textile workshop for a short time. She had long worked with the last Bauhaus director, Ludwig Mies van der Rohe, and had made a name for herself with her extravagant interior designs. The textile workshop, despite the mocking, was one of the Bauhaus' most financially successful workshops.

Textilwerkstatt „Wo Wolle ist, ist auch ein Weib das webt, und sei es nur zum Zeitvertreib", spöttelte Oskar Schlemmer, denn in Weimar stand die Textilwerkstatt noch stark in der Tradition „kunstgewerblicher Frauenarbeit". Hier wurde geknüpft, gestickt, genäht und gewebt, wobei sich die jungen Frauen die technischen Fähigkeiten des Webens weitgehend selbst beibringen mussten. Es entstanden Wandteppiche mit erzählenden Motiven, aber auch abstrakte Webexperimente. Die Weberei war stets eine der größten Werkstätten des Bauhauses, nicht zuletzt, weil fast alle Frauen dieser Werkstatt zugewiesen wurden.

In Dessau war zunächst der Maler Georg Muche Formmeister, aber mit Gunta Stölzl bekam die Weberei 1927 die erste Jungmeisterin des Bauhauses. Das Profil der Werkstatt, die im ersten Obergeschoss eingerichtet wurde, änderte sich, und in der modernisierten Abteilung wurden nun Muster für die Industrie, vor allem Gebrauchsstoffe, entwickelt. Experimente mit neuen Fasern wie zum Beispiel Cellophan führten zu ganz neuen Stoffqualitäten: Schall schluckende, Licht reflektierende oder besonders haltbare Stoffe entstanden.

Die Entwicklung von Stahlrohrmöbeln machte neue Bespannungen notwendig, denn die üblichen Rosshaar- und Baumwollstoffe hielten der höheren Belastung durch die fehlende Polsterung nicht stand. Die Weberinnen des Bauhauses entwickelten daher Ende der 20er Jahre einen speziellen, extrem haltbaren Spannstoff, das so genannte Eisengarngewebe. 1928 konnten die Kunden in einem Vertriebskatalog von Breuer-Möbeln erstmals zwischen schwarzem, rostfarbenem und grauem Bezug wählen, und in den 30er Jahren war Eisengarn als Möbelbespannung gängig.

1932 übernahm die Innenarchitektin Lilly Reich für kurze Zeit die Textilwerkstatt. Sie arbeitete schon länger mit dem letzten Bauhaus-Direktor Ludwig Mies van der Rohe zusammen und hatte sich mit ihren extravaganten Innenarchitekturen einen Namen gemacht. Die Weberei war trotz aller Spötteleien eine der finanziell erfolgreichsten Werkstätten des Bauhauses.

Grete Reichardt, Teppich für ein Kinderzimmer, 1929 entworfen, 1977 hergestellt
Grete Reichardt, carpet for a child's room, designed 1929, manufactured 1977

Tischlerei Möbel am Bauhaus – damit verbindet man heute meist die Stahlrohrmöbel von Marcel Breuer, wie zum Beispiel den Klubsessel B3. Dabei spielte Metall in der Tischlerei immer nur eine untergeordnete Rolle, die meisten Möbel wurden stets aus Holz gefertigt.

In Weimar leitete Walter Gropius die Werkstatt von 1922 bis 1925 selbst. Praktisch und vielseitig sollten die Einrichtungen sein, und es entstanden einfache Kastenmöbel in hoher Qualität. Schon früh wurde in der Tischlerei über eine Typisierung der Modelle nachgedacht, vor allem von Marcel Breuer. In Dessau übernahm er als Jungmeister die Tischlerei im Erdgeschoss des Werkstattflügels und verwendete unter anderem Stahlrohr für seine Entwürfe. Seine Modelle waren für die industrielle Produktion gedacht, wurden jedoch zunächst nur in Kleinserien gefertigt. Seine Stühle und Sessel waren deshalb teuer und für Kleinverdiener kaum erschwinglich.

Trotzdem wurde der Stahlrohrsessel „Wassily" ein Bauhausklassiker: klare, geometrische Formen, freiliegende Konstruktion, Reduktion auf die wesentliche Funktion, keine Schnörkel. Von seinem Gestalter Marcel Breuer „Klubsessel B3" getauft, bekam er den werbeträchtigen Namen „Wassily" erst in den 1960er Jahren von einer italienischen Firma, die den Entwurf nachbaute. Angeblich war es Wassily Kandinsky, der als einer der Ersten ein Exemplar erwarb.

Carpentry workshop Furniture at the Bauhaus: Today, this is usually associated with Marcel Breuer's tubular steel furniture, for example the Club Chair B3. Metal, however, always played a subordinate role in the carpentry, as most of the furniture was made of wood.

From 1922 to 1925, Walter Gropius was in charge of the workshop in Weimar. The furniture was to be practical and versatile, and simple, freestanding cabinets were made to high standards. In the carpentry, the standardisation of prototypes quickly became important, especially for Marcel Breuer. In Dessau as a Junior Master, he took charge of the carpentry workshop on the ground floor of the workshop wing and used tubular steel, among other things, in his designs. Although his prototypes were intended for industrial reproduction, they were first produced in small series. His chairs and armchairs were therefore expensive and rarely affordable for low earners.

Nevertheless, the "Wassily" tubular steel chair became a Bauhaus classic: simple, geometric forms, exposed structure, reduction to the essential function, no adornment. Christened "Club Chair B3" by its designer, Marcel Breuer, it was first given the commercial name "Wassily" in the 1960s by an Italian firm making reproductions of the chair. Apparently, Wassily Kandinsky was one of the first to buy the chair. According to Breuer, "these pieces of metal furniture should be no more than the necessary apparatus of modern life" ("metallmöbel und moderne räumlichkeiten", 1928). Compared with the comfortable upholstered furniture of the period, the B3 seems very futuristic indeed – and this is maybe why it still seems so modern today. Breuer reduced the load-bearing structure to a minimum, and used narrow strips of material for the seat and the arm and back rests. The chair weighed six kilogrammes, around a quarter of the weight of a traditional arm-chair. Although origi-

Marcel Breuer, Clubsessel, Prototyp des späteren B3, 1925/26
Marcel Breuer, Club Chair, early prototype of the B3, 1925/26

Carl Fieger, Schlafzimmereinrichtung für Haus Fieger, 1927
Carl Fieger, bedroom furniture
for the Fieger house, 1927

nally located elsewhere, it may be seen today in the entrance hall of the Bauhaus Building.

The wooden furniture designed at the same time was less spectacular, but easier to produce. From 1928 on, particularly when Hannes Meyer was director, work at the Bauhaus was geared to "people's needs" rather than "luxury goods". He merged the wood, metal and wall painting workshops to form a construction department, and Alfred Arndt became the new head of the carpentry workshop. Inexpensive folding furniture for small apartments was produced here alongside standard furniture for schools, thereby thoroughly redeeming the Bauhaus' social aspirations.

„Diese Metallmöbel sollen nichts weiter als notwendige Apparate heutigen Lebens sein", so Breuer selbst („metallmöbel und moderne räumlichkeiten", 1928). Verglichen mit gemütlichen Polstersesseln der Zeit erscheint der B3 in der Tat sehr maschinenhaft – und wirkt vielleicht deshalb heute noch so modern. Breuer reduzierte die Tragkonstruktion auf ein Minimum und nahm dünne Stoffbahnen für Sitz und Lehnen. Sechs Kilogramm wog sein Möbel, nur rund ein Viertel eines traditionellen Sessels. Er ist heute in den Foyers im Bauhausgebäude zu sehen, wo er ursprünglich allerdings nicht stand.

Die gleichzeitig entstandenen Entwürfe aus Holz waren vielleicht weniger spektakulär, aber leichter zu produzieren. Besonders unter Hannes Meyer als Direktor wurde im Bauhaus ab 1928 für den „Volksbedarf" gearbeitet, nicht für den „Luxusbedarf". Er legte die Holz-, Metall und Wandmalereiwerkstatt zur Ausbauabteilung zusammen, und neuer Leiter der Tischlerei wurde Alfred Arndt. Hier entstanden preiswerte Klappmöbel für kleine Wohnungen und Typenmöbel für Schulen, die den sozialen Anspruch des Bauhauses durchaus einlösten.

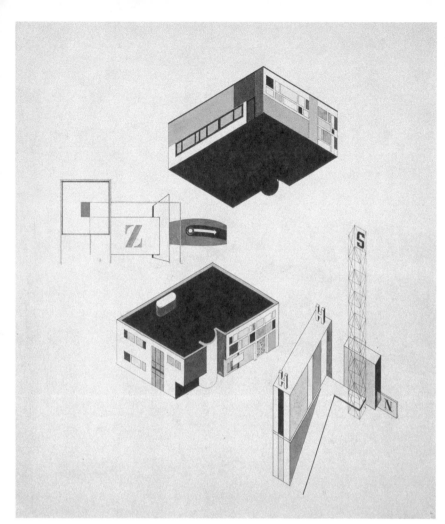

Franz Ehrlich, Architekturentwurf mit
farbiger Wandgestaltung, um 1930
Franz Ehrlich, Architectural draft with
coloured wall design, ca. 1930

Wandmalereiwerkstatt Das Bauhaus wurde vor allem in den ersten Jahren maßgeblich durch die Zusammenarbeit von Architekten und Malern geprägt, und besonders stark beeinflussten sich diese Disziplinen in der Werkstatt für Wandmalerei. In Weimar wurden noch großformatige, dekorative Wandbilder gefertigt; in Dessau hingegen verstärkte sich der Einfluss der Konstruktivisten. Die Farbe betonte nun die Architektur und konstituierte Raum, statt ihn zu dekorieren.

Der junge Malermeister Hinnerk Scheper übernahm die Werkstatt im zweiten Obergeschoss. Er baute eine differenzierte theoretische und praktische Ausbildung auf und experimentierte mit neuen Techniken. Entgegen der heute gängigen Meinung, das Bauhaus sei weitgehend unbunt, gestaltete Scheper das Bauhausgebäude innen farbig aus. „Bei der Gestaltung werden tragende und füllende Flächen unterschieden und dadurch deren architektonische Spannung zum klaren Ausdruck gebracht. Die räumliche Wirkung der Farbe wird gesteigert durch Anwendung verschiedener Materialien: glatte, polierte, körnige und rauhe Putzflächen, matte, stumpfe und glänzende Anstriche, Glas, Metall usw." (Hinnerk Scheper, 1926) Von typischen Bauhausfarben – Rot, Gelb, Blau – kann nach heutiger Kenntnis keine Rede sein. Schaut man sich in den Bauhausbauten in Dessau um, so stellt man fest, dass eigentlich jede Farbe eine Bauhausfarbe ist.

Untersuchungen ergaben, dass der von Scheper entwickelte Farbplan für das Bauhausgebäude zu ca. 80 Prozent umgesetzt wurde. Die Rekonstruktion stellte die Restauratoren vor eine schwierige Aufgabe, denn es wurden kaum fertige Farben verwendet, sondern diese mit Pigmenten gemischt und abgetönt. So stellte heute jede Wand ein Unikat dar, das detailgenau wiederhergestellt worden ist.

Wall painting workshop Particularly in the early years, the Bauhaus was hugely influenced by the collaboration between architects and painters, and the influence of these disciplines was particularly marked in the wall painting workshop. In Weimar, large-format, decorative murals were still being produced; in Dessau, however, the influence of the constructivists grew. Colour now enhanced architecture, and it constituted, rather than decorated, space.

The young painting Master Hinnerk Scheper took charge of the workshop on the second floor. He developed a distinct theoretical and practical approach to teaching, and experimented with new techniques. Contrary to the conventional view of the Bauhaus as largely monochromatic, Scheper designed a colourful interior for the Bauhaus Building. "There is a clear distinction between the designs of load-bearing and in-filling surfaces, thereby bringing their architectonic tension to the fore. The spatial effect of the colour is increased by the use of different materials: smooth, polished, granular and rough plaster surfaces, matt, dull and glossy paints, glass, metal, etc." (Hinnerk Scheper, 1926). Bearing in mind what we know today, there can be no question of "typical" (red, yellow and blue) Bauhaus colours. If one looks around the Bauhaus buildings in Dessau, one sees that, by rights, all colours are Bauhaus colours.

Research shows that approximately 80 percent of Hinnerk Scheper's colour design for the Bauhaus Building was realised. Its reconstruction was a difficult task for the restorers: ready-mixed colours were rarely used, as these were mixed with pigments to create different shades. Today, each wall is therefore a unique specimen – a reconstruction accurate in every detail. The element of colour design was enhanced by a second – the Bauhaus wallpaper – that was developed in 1929 and became the school's most successful product. A contemporary advertisement states: "bauhaus wallpapers are the pioneers of good taste. they are suitable for every home, are conservatively patterned, and may be bought in every good wallpaper shop in 250 matching shades. unrivalled quality and value for money". The evolution of the Bauhaus wallpaper was closely associated with housing construction in the 20s. The New Architecture housing estates built across Germany were promoted under the motto of "Light, air, sun". Boldly patterned, brightly coloured wallpapers were no longer suitable for the small rooms, which were to be far less representational than functional. In autumn 1929, the first sample card was produced, showing 14 different cross-hatched and dotted patterns and structures. This also put one of Hinnerk Scheper's ideas into practice: to transfer the wall colours and surface effects developed at the Bauhaus from plaster to paper, and make this available to the general public.

Neben der Farbe als Gestaltungselement wurde 1929 die Bauhaus-Tapete entwickelt, das erfolgreichste Produkt der Schule. „bauhaus-tapeten sind wegweiser des guten geschmacks. sie passen in jedes heim, sind zurückhaltend gemustert und in 250 aufeinander abgestimmten farbtönen in jeder besseren tapetenhandlung zu erhalten. qualität und preiswürdigkeit sind unübertroffen" – so hieß es in einer zeitgenössischen Werbung. Die Entwicklung der Bauhaus-Tapete war eng verknüpft mit dem Wohnungsbau der 1920er Jahre. „Licht – Luft – Sonne" war das Motto, unter dem in ganz Deutschland Siedlungen des Neuen Bauens entstanden. Groß gemusterte, stark farbige Tapeten waren nicht mehr angemessen für die kleinen Räume, die weniger repräsentativ als vielmehr funktional sein sollten. Ab Herbst 1929 gab es die erste Musterkarte mit 14 unterschiedlichen Schraffuren, Strichelungen und Strukturen. Damit wurde auch eine Idee von Hinnerk Scheper verwirklicht: die vom Bauhaus entwickelte Wandfarbigkeit und Oberflächenwirkung von Putz auf Papier zu übertragen und breiten Bevölkerungsschichten zugänglich zu machen.

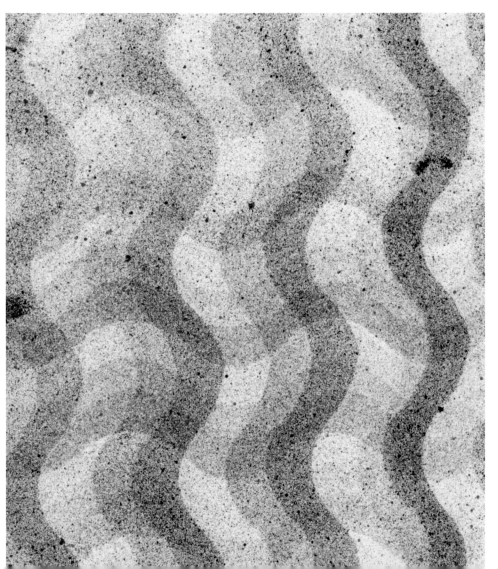

Grete Reichardt, Tapetenentwurf, um 1930
Grete Reichardt, wallpaper design, ca. 1930

Bauhaus und Bauhäusler
nach 1932/33

Bauhaus and Bauhaus people
after 1932/33

Bauhaus people The Masters and students experienced varied fates after the school's closure in 1933. From 1937, a number of the teachers, among them Wassily Kandinsky and Paul Klee, were defamed as "degenerate" by the National Socialists. Many, such as Oskar Schlemmer, were prohibited from working. Others, such as Josef and Anni Albers, emigrated. Yet others, such as Marianne Brandt, withdrew completely into private life.

The Jewish Bauhaus associates, including Otti Berger and Friedl Dicker, died in concentration camps. Most of the students were unknown to the public, however, and were not targeted by the National Socialists' anti-Bauhaus propaganda. Many were able to continue with the careers that they had begun in industry, trade or construction.

The Bauhaus concept was kept alive by its Masters and students and was spread across the world, above all by the emigrants. The following examples merely indicate this development: Josef and Anni Albers moved in 1933 to Ashville, North Carolina, USA to become professors at Black Mountain College. The most successful students here later included John Cage, Cy Twombly and Robert Rauschenberg. László Moholy-Nagy was entrusted by the Association of Arts and Industries with the foundation of the New Bauhaus in Chicago, Illinois, USA, where he was to replace the prevailing Beaux Arts tradition with modern teaching methods and to establish a new basis for production design. In 1935/36, Walter Gropius was initially self-employed as an architect in England. In 1937, he was appointed professor at the Harvard Graduate School of Design in Cambridge, Massachusetts, USA. Marcel Breuer and Herbert Bayer also moved to the New England states in the USA. Ludwig Mies van der Rohe, Ludwig Hilberseimer and Walter Peterhans had a great influence on teaching at the Illinois Institute of Technology in Chicago, Illinois, USA for many years.

Attempts to revive the Bauhaus concept were also made in West and East Germany. In 1953 in the new west German Federal Republic (FRG), the Hochschule für Gestaltung (HfG) was opened in Ulm. The building's architect and first principal was Max Bill, a former student of the Bauhaus, and guest lecturers included, among many others, Josef Albers and Johannes Itten. Many of the Bauhaus' teachers and students taught in the Federal Republic's newly established exterior and interior architecture schools and art schools (e.g., Else Mögelin, Otto Lindig and Gerhard Marcks at the Landeskunstschule Hamburg). Former directors of the Bauhaus designed outstanding buildings, including Ludwig Mies van der Rohe's Neue Nationalgalerie in Berlin.

In 1960, the foundation by Hans Maria Wingler of the Bauhaus Archive in Darmstadt (today the Bauhaus Archive/Museum of Design in Berlin) institutionalised the collection and research of Bauhaus objects in West Germany. In 1968, a large Bauhaus exhibition was held in Stuttgart. This was designed, among others, by Ludwig Grote und Herbert Bayer, and was deemed a great success worldwide.

Even before the German Democratic Republic (GDR) was established in the eastern part of Germany, attempts by former

Bauhäusler Die weiteren Lebenswege der Lehrenden und Studierenden verliefen nach Schließung der Schule 1933 sehr unterschiedlich. Zahlreiche Lehrer wurden seit 1937 von den Nationalsozialisten als „entartet" diffamiert, unter anderen Wassily Kandinsky und Paul Klee. Viele erhielten, wie Oskar Schlemmer, Berufsverbot, oder sie emigrierten, wie Josef und Anni Albers. Andere zogen sich völlig ins Privatleben zurück, zum Beispiel Marianne Brandt. Jüdische Bauhäusler wurden in Konzentrationslagern umgebracht, unter ihnen Otti Berger und Friedl Dicker. Die Mehrzahl der Studierenden jedoch war in der Öffentlichkeit weitgehend unbekannt und kein Ziel der nationalsozialistischen Anti-Bauhaus-Propaganda. Viele konnten ihre begonnene Laufbahn in Industrie, Handwerk oder Bauwesen fortsetzen.

Die Idee des Bauhauses blieb durch ihre Lehrer und Schüler lebendig und wurde, gerade auch durch die Emigranten, in die ganze Welt getragen. Die folgenden Beispiele sollen diese Entwicklung nur andeuten: Josef und Anni Albers gingen gleich 1933 als Lehrer nach Ashville, North Carolina/USA an das Black Mountain College, zu dessen bekanntesten Schülern später u.a. John Cage, Cy Twombly oder Robert Rauschenberg gehörten. László Moholy-Nagy wurde 1937 von der Association of Arts and Industries mit der Gründung des New Bauhaus in Chicago, Illinois/USA betraut, um die bis dahin geltende Beaux-Arts-Tradition durch moderne Lehrmethoden zu ersetzen und die Produktgestaltung auf eine neue Grundlage zu stellen. Walter Gropius war 1935/36 zunächst als Privatarchitekt in England tätig und wurde 1937 als Professor an die Harvard Graduate School of Design in Cambridge, Massachusetts/USA berufen, und auch Marcel Breuer und Herbert Bayer gingen in die Neuenglandstaaten der USA. Ludwig Mies van der Rohe, Ludwig Hilberseimer und Walter Peterhans prägten über Jahre die Lehre am Illinois Institute of Technology in Chicago, Illinois/USA.

Auch in West- und Ostdeutschland gab es Wiederbelebungsversuche der Bauhaus-Idee. 1953 wurde in der jungen Bundesrepublik die Hochschule für Gestaltung (HfG) Ulm eröffnet. Architekt des Gebäudes und erster Rektor war der Bauhäusler Max Bill, und zu den Gastdozenten gehörten neben vielen anderen Josef Albers und Johannes Itten. Zahlreiche Bauhausschülerinnen und -schüler lehrten nach dem Krieg in den neu gegründeten Werkkunst- und Kunstschulen der Bundesrepublik (z.B. Else Mögelin, Otto Lindig und Gerhard Marcks an der Landeskunstschule Hamburg). Ehemalige Bauhausdirektoren schufen herausragende Bauten, z.B. Ludwig Mies van der Rohe die Neue Nationalgalerie in Berlin.

Mit der Gründung des Bauhaus-Archivs in Darmstadt unter Hans Maria Wingler 1960 (heute Bauhaus-Archiv Museum für Gestaltung, Berlin) wurde die Sammlung und Erforschung von Bauhausobjekten in der Bundesrepublik institutionalisiert. 1968 fand eine große Bauhaus-Ausstellung in Stuttgart statt, die unter anderen von Ludwig Grote und Herbert Bayer konzipiert wurde und weltweit großen Erfolg hatte.

Noch vor Gründung der DDR scheiterten Wiederbelebungsversuche des Bauhauses durch ehemalige Bauhäusler in Dessau an den veränderten politischen Rahmenbedingungen in der Sowjetischen Besatzungszone (SBZ). 1950 ging die DDR im Zuge der so genannten Formalismusdebatte deutlich auf Distanz zum Bauhaus. Nach einer Reise von Architekten in die Sowjetunion wurde der neue Kurs definiert, der eine Architektur vorsah, die in einer „nationalen Tradition" stehen und sich unter anderem an einen vereinfachten Klassizismus anlehnen sollte. Bauhäusler wie Richard Paulick, Franz Ehrlich oder Edmund Collein prägten die Stadtentwicklung, die Architektur und das Design der DDR bis in die frühen 1970er Jahre ganz entscheidend mit. Andere, wie Marianne Brandt und Mart Stam, konnten nach 1950 nur kurze Zeit als Dozenten an den Hochschulen in Dresden und Berlin-Weißensee lehren. Einige Bauhäusler konnten jedoch in der DDR ihr Leben lang Impulse aus dem Bauhaus durch ihre Lehrtätigkeit vermitteln, wie Selman Selmanagic in Berlin, Walter Funkat in Halle/Saale oder Peter Keler und Konrad Püschel in Weimar.

Bereits 1963 wurde in der DDR wieder positiv über die Avantgarde-Schule publiziert, und seit 1967 fanden in Dessau und Weimar Bauhaus-Ausstellungen statt. Eine weitere Öffnung des gesellschaftlichen Lebens Anfang der 70er Jahre führte zu einer grundlegend anderen Haltung gegenüber dem Bauhauserbe und machte 1976 die erste denkmalgerechte Rekonstruktion des Bauhausgebäudes möglich.

Bauhaus people to revive the Bauhaus in Dessau failed, due to the prevailing political climate in the Soviet Occupation Zone. In 1950, in the course of the so-called "formalism debate", the GDR distanced itself from the Bauhaus. Following a trip taken by architects to the Soviet Union, a new direction was defined, which envisaged an architecture based on "national traditions", and which was to be modelled on a simplified form of Classicism. Bauhaus associates such as Richard Paulick, Franz Ehrlich and Edmund Collein had a strong influence on urban development, architecture and design in the GDR until the early 1970s. After 1950, others, such as Marianne Brandt and Mart Stam, were only able to hold short-term posts as lecturers at high schools in Dresden and Berlin-Weißensee. However, some of the Bauhaus people were able, throughout their lives in the GDR, to pass on the Bauhaus concepts in their teaching. These included Selman Selmanagic in Berlin, Walter Funkat in Halle/Saale, and Peter Keler and Konrad Püschel in Weimar.

In the GDR, by 1963 the avant-garde school had a positive public profile again and, from 1967, Bauhaus exhibitions were held in Dessau and Weimar. A new policy of openness, which was applied to social issues in the early 1970s, led to a fundamental change in attitudes to the Bauhaus legacy, and this made the restoration of the Bauhaus Building (in line with the precepts of monument conservation) possible for the first time.

Bauhaus Building On 1st October 1932, the staff and students at the Bauhaus were forced to leave their school in Dessau when the municipal council ordered the institution's closure. The vocational school was permitted to stay in the north wing. The Bauhaus Building was then managed by the municipal building authorities, and other educational institutions, such as a home economics school and a National Socialist "Gau" school, moved in. In 1938, the meanwhile nationalised Junkers factory had their offices here, as did, probably in the 1940s, the Minister for Armaments, Albert Speer.

During the second large-scale air raid on Dessau on 7th March 1945, the Bauhaus too was hit. The festive area was extensively damaged by fire; the glass curtain wall was destroyed by the heat and most of it had to be removed. The walls of the workshop wing were provisionally repaired with brick and fitted with simple windows: every available space in the city, 80 percent of which had been destroyed, had to be put to use. The Bauhaus Building was first occupied by a hospital and then by vocational schools, which urgently required space.

Around 1960, the provisional brick walls of the workshop wing were refitted with rows of windows in the aesthetic style of the north wing. In 1964, under the guidance of the former Bauhaus associate Konrad Püschel, a survey of the building was carried out by students at the Hochschule für Architektur und Bauwesen (HAB) in Weimar. In 1974, the building was included on the GDR's main monument register, and the decision was made to restore the building. In 1976, on the building's 50th anniversary, the first restoration of the building, carried out in line with the precepts of monument conservation, was largely complete. The vocational school, with its business, trade and medical departments, continued to use the space, and the ground floor of the workshop wing served temporarily as a gymnasium. In 1976, a scientific and cultural centre was also set up, and work began on the development of an art and design collection and an archive. Ten years later, the Bauhaus became the Zentrum für Gestaltung der DDR (GDR centre of design). Since 1994, after the renunification, the Bauhaus Dessau Foundation has been the owner and occupier of the building. Every year, around 80,000 people from all over the world interested in architecture and art visit the building in order to explore, and be inspired by, this UNESCO World Heritage Site.

Bauhausgebäude Zum 1. Oktober 1932 mussten die Bauhäusler ihre Schule in Dessau räumen, nachdem der Gemeinderat die Schließung der Institution verfügt hatte. Die Gewerbliche Berufsschule konnte weitgehend im Nordflügel verbleiben. Das Bauhausgebäude wurde danach vom Stadtbauamt verwaltet, und mit einer Hauswirtschaftsschule sowie einer „Amtswalterschule der NSDAP" zogen später andere Lehranstalten ein. Ab 1938 hatten hier auch die inzwischen verstaatlichten Junkerswerke und in den 40er Jahren vermutlich Albert Speer als Rüstungsminister ihre Büros.

Beim zweiten großen Bombenangriff auf Dessau am 7. März 1945 wurde auch das Bauhaus getroffen. Die Festebene brannte weitgehend aus, die Glasvorhangfassade wurde durch die Hitzeentwicklung zerstört und musste fast vollständig abgenommen werden. Die Wände des Werkstattflügels wurden notdürftig aufgemauert und mit Barackenfenstern versehen – in der zu über 80 Prozent zerstörten Stadt musste jeder verfügbare Raum genutzt werden. Ins Bauhausgebäude zogen erst ein Lazarett und dann Berufsschulen ein, die dringend Raum benötigten.

Um 1960 wurden anstelle der provisorischen Ziegelwände des Werkstattflügels Fensterbänder eingezogen, die sich an die Ästhetik des Nordflügels anlehnten. Unter Leitung des ehemaligen Bauhäuslers Konrad Püschel wurde 1964 das Gebäude von Studierenden der Hochschule für Architektur und Bauwesen (HAB) Weimar aufgemessen. 1974 erfolgten die Aufnahme auf die zentrale Denkmalliste der DDR und der Beschluss zur Wiederherstellung. 1976, zum 50. Geburtstag des Gebäudes, war die erste denkmalgerechte Rekonstruktion des Bauhauses in großen Teilen abgeschlossen. Die Berufsschule mit ihrem gewerblichen, kaufmännischen und medizinischen Zweig nutzte die Räumlichkeiten weiter, und zeitweilig diente das Erdgeschoss des Werkstattflügels als Turnhalle. 1976 wurde zudem ein „Wissenschaftlich-Kulturelles Zentrum" eingerichtet, und der Aufbau einer Kunst- und Designsammlung sowie eines Archivs begann. Zehn Jahre später wurde das Bauhaus zum „Zentrum für Gestaltung der DDR".

Seit 1994 ist die Stiftung Bauhaus Dessau Eigentümerin und Nutzerin des Gebäudes. Rund 80.000 architektur- und kunstinteressierte Besucher aus aller Welt kommen jedes Jahr, um dieses UNESCO Welterbe der Menschheit zu erkunden und sich in seinen Bann ziehen zu lassen.

Biographies Kurzporträts

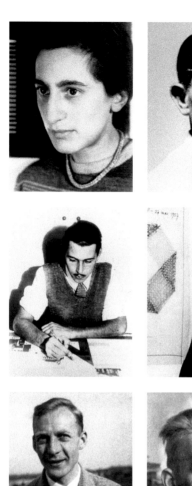

von links nach rechts (linke Seite) from left to right (left page):
Anni Albers I Josef Albers I Alfred Arndt I Gertrud Arndt
Herbert Bayer I Max Bill I Marianne Brandt I Marcel Breuer
Edmund Collein I Erich Consemüller I Franz Ehrlich I Lyonel Feininger
Carl Fieger I Walter Gropius I Ludwig Grote I Fritz Hesse
Ludwig Hilberseimer

von links nach rechts (rechte Seite) from left to right (right page):
Johannes Itten I Hugo Junkers I Wassily Kandinsky I Paul Klee
Max Krajewski I Hannes Meyer I Ludwig Mies van der Rohe I Lucia Moholy
László Moholy-Nagy I Georg Muche I Richard Paulick I Walter Peterhans
Lilly Reich I Grete Reichardt I Xanti Schawinski I Hinnerk Scheper
Oskar Schlemmer I Joost Schmidt I Gunta Stölzl I Wilhelm Wagenfeld

Anni Albers, geb. Fleischmann (1899–1994) Weberin, Designerin, 1899 in Berlin geboren. 1916–19 Malerei- und Kunstgewerbestudium in Hamburg. 1922 Immatrikulation am Staatlichen Bauhaus Weimar, Vorkurs bei Johannes Itten und Lehre in der Webereiwerkstatt bei Georg Muche. Experimente mit ungewöhnlichen Materialien. Künstlerische Gestaltungslehre bei Wassily Kandinsky und Paul Klee. Ab 1927 Lehre in der Weberei bei Gunta Stölzl, 1928 stellvertretende Leiterin der Werkstatt. Herstellung von schalldämpfenden Stoffen für die Aula der Bundesschule des Allgemeinen Deutschen Gewerkschaftsbundes in Bernau bei Berlin. 1930 Bauhaus-Diplom, 1931 kommissarische Leiterin der Weberei. 1931 Preis der Stadt Berlin auf der Deutschen Bauausstellung. 1933 Emigration in die USA, bis 1949 Assistant Professor of Art am Black Mountain College in Ashville, North Carolina. 1949 Übersiedlung nach New York, Einzelausstellung im Museum of Modern Art in New York. Ab 1950 freie Weberein in New Haven, Connecticut, Lehrtätigkeit in den USA, Europa und Japan. Seit den 1960er Jahren Beschäftigung mit abstrakter Grafik. 1994 in Orange, Connecticut gestorben.

Anni Albers, born Fleischmann (1899–1994) Weaver, designer, Born 1899 in Berlin. 1916–19 Studied painting and applied arts and crafts in Hamburg. 1922 Enrolment at the Staatliche Bauhaus Weimar, preliminary course under Johannes Itten, apprenticeship in the textile workshop under Georg Muche. Experimentation with unusual materials. Tuition in artistic design theory under Wassily Kandinsky and Paul Klee. From 1927 Apprenticeship in the textile workshop under Gunta Stölzl, 1928 acting head of the workshop. Manufacture of sound insulation materials for the auditorium of the Bundesschule des Allgemeinen Deutschen Gewerkschaftsbundes in Bernau near Berlin. 1930 Bauhaus diploma, 1931 Provisional head of the textile workshop. 1931 Awarded the Berlin Prize at the Deutsche Bauausstellung. 1933 Emigration to the USA. To 1949 Assistant Professor of Art at Black Mountain College in Ashville, North Carolina. 1949 Relocation to New York, exhibition at the Museum of Modern Art in New York. From 1950 Freelance weaver in New Haven, Connecticut, teaching in the USA, Europe and Japan. From 1960 Pursuit of abstract graphics. Died 1994 in Orange, Connecticut.

Josef Albers (1888–1976) Maler, Grafiker, Designer, Kunstpädagoge, 1888 in Bottrop geboren. Ab 1905 Ausbildung zum Volkschullehrer. 1919 Kunststudium an der Münchner Akademie bei Franz von Stuck. 1920 Immatrikulation am Staatlichen Bauhaus Weimar, 1920–21 Vorkurs bei Johannes Itten. 1921–23 Glasmalereiwerkstatt bei Johannes Itten. 1923–25 Geselle und Werkmeister der Glasmalereiwerkstatt, Lehrer des Vorkurses. 1925–32 Leiter des Vorkurses am Bauhaus Dessau, bis 1928 gemeinsam mit László Moholy-Nagy. 1925–28 Leitung der Tischlereiwerkstatt. 1932–33 Leiter des Vorkurses und Lehrer für Zeichnen und Schrift am Bauhaus in Berlin. 1933 Emigration in die USA, bis 1949 Kunstprofessor am Black Mountain College in Ashville, North Carolina.

Schüler waren u. a. Willem de Kooning und Robert Rauschenberg. Nach 1936 Gastprofessuren in aller Welt. 1950 Berufung zum Direktor des Departments of Design der Yale University School of Arts in New Haven, Connecticut. Fertigung der Serien „Strukturale Konstellationen" und „Huldigung an das Quadrat". 1976 in Orange, Connecticut gestorben.

Josef Albers (1888–1976) Painter, graphic designer, designer, art teacher, Born 1888 in Bottrop. From 1905 Trained as an elementary school teacher. 1919 Studied art at the Münchner Akademie under Franz von Stuck. 1920 Enrolment at the Staatliche Bauhaus Weimar, 1920–21 Preliminary course under Johannes Itten. 1921–23 Glass painting workshop under Johannes Itten. 1923–25 Journeyman and Technical Master in the glass–painting workshop, preliminary course tutor. 1925–32 Head of the preliminary course at the Bauhaus in Dessau, jointly with László Moholy-Nagy until 1928. 1925–28 Head of the carpentry workshop. 1932–33 Head of the preliminary course and drawing and calligraphy tutor at the Bauhaus in Berlin. 1933 Emigration to the USA. To 1949 Professor of Art at Black Mountain College in Ashville, North Carolina. Students included Willem de Kooning and Robert Rauschenberg. From 1936 Guest professorships worldwide. 1950 Appointment as director of the Department of Design at Yale University School of Arts in New Haven, Connecticut. Created the series "Structural Constellations" and "Homages to the Square". Died 1976 in Orange, Connecticut.

Alfred Arndt (1898–1976) Maler, Zeichner, Architekt, 1898 in Elbing geboren. Zeichenlehre, 1920–21 Gewerbeschule Elbing, 1921 Kunstakademie Königsberg. 1921 Immatrikulation am Staatlichen Bauhaus Weimar, Vorkurs bei Johannes Itten, Unterricht bei Paul Klee. 1922–25 Wandmalereiwerkstatt bei Wassily Kandinsky, 1924 Gesellenprüfung vor der Handwerkskammer Weimar. 1925–28 am Bauhaus Dessau Wandmalereiwerkstatt bei Hinnerk Scheper, 1926–28 Tischlereiwerkstatt bei Marcel Breuer. 1928 Meisterprüfung, bis 1929 freier Architekt in Probstzella/Thüringen. 1929–30 Leiter der Ausbauwerkstatt am Bauhaus Dessau, 1930–31 Leiter der Abteilung Bau und Ausbau. 1931–32 Lehrer in Ausbaukonstruktion, Darstellender Geometrie und Perspektive. 1932 Umzug nach Probstzella, bis 1945 freier Architekt und Werbegrafiker, Architekt in Thüringer Industrieunternehmen. 1945–47 Leitung des Hochbau- und Planungsamtes der Stadt Jena. 1948 Übersiedlung nach Darmstadt, Berater beim Aufbau des Bauhaus-Archivs. 1976 in Darmstadt gestorben.

Alfred Arndt (1898–1976) Painter, draughtsman, architect, Born 1898 in Elbing. Apprenticeship as a draughtsman. 1920–21 Gewerbeschule Elbing, 1921 Kunstakademie Königsberg. 1921 Enrolment at the Staatliche Bauhaus Weimar, preliminary course under Johannes Itten, tuition with Paul Klee. 1922–25 Wall painting workshop with Wassily Kandinsky, 1924 Journeyman's certificate from the chamber of trade in Weimar. 1925–28 At the Bauhaus in Dessau, wall painting workshop under Hinnerk Scheper, 1926–28 carpentry workshop under Marcel Breuer. 1928 Master's certificate. To 1929 Freelance architect in Probstzella, Thuringia. 1929–30 Head of the construction workshop at the Bauhaus in Dessau. 1930–31 Head of the department of architecture and construction. 1931–32 Tutor in construction, descriptive geometry and perspective. 1932 Relocation to Probstzella. To 1945 Freelance architect and commercial artist, architect for industrial firms in Thuringia. 1945–47 Head of the municipal structural engineering and planning department in Jena. 1948 Relocation to Darmstadt, consultant for the development of the Bauhaus Archive. Died 1976 in Darmstadt.

Gertrud Arndt, geb. Hantschk (1903–2000) Weberin, Fotografin, 1903 in Ratibor/Oberschlesien geboren. 1919–22 Architekturausbildung in Erfurt, Besuch der Kunstgewerbeschule. 1923 Immatrikulation am Staatlichen Bauhaus Weimar, Vorkurs bei László Moholy-Nagy, Unterricht bei Wassily Kandinsky und Paul Klee. 1924–1925 Webereiwerkstatt bei Georg Muche, Unterricht bei Adolf Meyer. 1925–27 am Bauhaus Dessau Webereiwerkstatt bei Georg Muche, bis 1928 bei Gunta Stölzl. 1927 Gesellenprüfung vor der Weberinnen in Sachsen. Umzug nach Probstzella/Thüringen. 1929 mit Alfred Arndt Einzug in die Meisterhäuser in Dessau, dort Einrichtung eines Fotolabors und Fertigung der „Maskenfotos". 1932 Umzug nach Probstzella. 1948 Übersiedlung nach Darmstadt, dort 2000 gestorben.

Gertrud Arndt, born Hantschk (1903–2000) Weaver, photographer, Born 1903 in Ratibor, Upper Silesia. 1919–22 Studied architecture in Erfurt, attended the Kunstgewerbeschule. 1923 Enrolment at the Staatliche Bauhaus Weimar, preliminary course under László Moholy-Nagy, tuition with Wassily Kandinsky and Paul Klee. 1924–1925 Textile workshop with Georg Muche, tuition with Adolf Meyer. 1925–27 At the Bauhaus in Dessau, textile workshop under Georg Muche, until 1928 under Gunta Stölzl. 1927 Journeyman's certificate from the weavers' guild in Saxony. Relocation to Probstzella, Thuringia. 1929 Moved into the Masters' Houses in Dessau with Alfred Arndt, establishing a photographic laboratory and creating the "Maskenfotos". 1932 Relocation to Probstzella. 1948 Relocation to Darmstadt, died there in 2000.

Herbert Bayer (1900–1985) Maler, Fotograf, Werbegrafiker, Typograf, Architekt, 1900 in Haag/Österreich geboren. 1919 Architekturausbildung in Linz. 1921 Immatrikulation am Staatlichen Bauhaus Weimar, Vorkurs bei Johannes Itten, Wandmalereiwerkstatt bei Wassily Kandinsky. 1925 Gesellenprüfung vor der Malerinnen in Weimar. 1925–28 am Bauhaus Dessau Jungmeister der Werkstatt für Druck und Reklame, Entwurf des Bauhaus-Schriftzuges, zahlreicher Geschäftsunterlagen und Prospekte, Einführung der Kleinschreibung. Ab 1928 Leiter der Werbeagentur Dorland in Berlin, Beschäftigung mit Malerei und Fotografie. Auch nach 1933 Ausstellungsgestaltung und Werbegrafik. 1938 Emigration nach New York und Gestaltung von Ausstellung und Katalog „Bauhaus 1919–1928" im Museum of Modern Art. Arbeit als Gestalter und Dozent. 1946 Übersiedlung nach Colorado, Arbeit als Architekt und Landschaftsgestalter. Künstlerischer Berater der „Container Corporation of America" und der „Atlantic Richfield Company". 1969 Gestaltung von Ausstellung und Katalog „50 Jahre Bauhaus" in Stuttgart. 1985 in Montecito, Kalifornien gestorben.

Herbert Bayer (1900–1985) Painter, photographer, commercial artist, typographer, architect, Born 1900 in Haag, Austria. 1919 Studied architecture in Linz. 1921 Enrolment at the Staatliche Bauhaus Weimar, preliminary course under Johannes Itten, wall painting workshop under Wassily Kandinsky. 1925 Journeyman's certificate from the painter's guild in Weimar. 1925–28 At the Bauhaus in Dessau, Junior Master of the painting and advertising workshops, design of the Bauhaus lettering and numerous business papers, leaflets and brochures, introduction of lower case lettering. From 1928 Head of the Dorland advertising agency in Berlin, pursuit of painting and photography. From 1933 Work in exhibition design and as a commercial artist. 1938 Emigration to New York, design of the exhibition and catalogue "Bauhaus 1919–1928" at the Museum of Modern Art. Work as a designer and lecturer. 1946 Relocation to Colorado, work as an architect and landscape designer. Artistic consultant for the Container Corporation of America and the Atlantic Richfield Company. 1969 Design of the exhibition and catalogue "50 Jahre Bauhaus" in Stuttgart. Died 1985 in Montecito, California.

Max Bill (1908–1994) Künstler, Designer, Architekt, 1908 in Winterthur/Schweiz geboren. 1924–27 Kunstgewerbeschule Zürich, Ausbildung zum Silberschmied. 1927 Immatrikulation am Bauhaus Dessau, Vorkurs und Metallwerkstatt bei László Moholy-Nagy, freie Malklasse bei Wassily Kandinsky und Paul Klee, Unterricht in der Bühnenwerkstatt und der Bauabteilung. 1929 Übersiedlung nach Zürich, tätig v. a. als Architekt, Maler, Grafiker, Plastiker. 1930 Beitritt zum Schweizerischer Werkbund, 1938 zum CIAM (Congrès International d'Architecture Moderne). 1944–45 Lehrauftrag für Formlehre an der von Johannes Itten geleiteten Kunstgewerbeschule Zürich. 1951 Mitbegründer und Erbauer der Hochschule für Gestaltung (HfG) Ulm, bis 1956 Rektor und Leiter der Abteilung Architektur und Produktform. 1957 Rückkehr in die Schweiz. 1967–74 Professor an der Staatlichen Hochschule für Bildende Künste in Hamburg, Lehrstuhl für Umweltgestaltung. 1994 in Berlin gestorben.

Max Bill (1908–1994) Artist, designer, architect, Born 1908 in Winterthur, Switzerland. 1924–27 Silversmith's apprenticeship at the Kunstgewerbeschule Zürich. 1927 Enrolment at the Bauhaus in Dessau, preliminary course and metal workshop under László Moholy-Nagy, free painting tuition with Wassily Kandinsky and Paul Klee, tuition in the theatre workshop and the department of architecture. 1929 Relocation to Zurich. Active as, among other things, architect, painter, graphic artist and sculptor. 1930 Admittance to the Swiss Werkbund and, in 1938, CIAM (Congrès International d'Architecture Moderne). 1944–45 Lectureships in product design at the Kunstgewerbeschule Zürich directed by Johannes Itten. 1951 Co-founder and director of the Hochschule für Gestaltung (HfG) in Ulm. To 1956 Principal and head of the department of architecture and product form. 1957 Return to Switzerland. 1967–74 Professor of environmental design at the Staatliche Hochschule fur Bildende Künste in Hamburg. 1994 Died in Berlin.

Marianne Brandt, geb. Liebe (1893–1983) Designerin, Malerin, Fotografin, 1893 in Chemnitz geboren. 1911–17 Studium der Malerei und Plastik an der Hochschule für Bildende Kunst in Weimar. 1920 Studienreise nach Frankreich. 1924 Immatrikulation am Staatlichen Bauhaus Weimar, Vorkurs bei Josef Albers und László Moholy-Nagy, Unterricht bei Paul Klee und Wassily Kandinsky. 1924–28 Metallwerkstatt bei László Moholy-Nagy in Weimar und Dessau. Leitung der lichttechnischen Versuche, zahlreiche Leuchtenentwürfe für die Bauhausbauten Dessau, teilweise gemeinsam mit Hin Bredendieck. 1928–1929 Leiterin der Metallwerkstatt am Bauhaus Dessau, Bauhaus-Diplom. Fertigung zahlreicher Fotografien und Collagen. 1929–30 Mitarbeiterin in Gropius' Berliner Büro, 1930–33 in der Metallwarenfabrik Ruppelwerke in Gotha. Nach 1933 arbeitslos. 1949–51 Dozentin an der Hochschule für Bildende Künste in Dresden, 1951–54 an der Hochschule für angewandte Kunst in Berlin-Weißensee. 1954 Rückzug ins Privatleben. 1983 in Kirchberg/Sachsen gestorben.

Marianne Brandt, born Liebe (1893–1983) Designer, painter, photographer, Born 1893 in Chemnitz. 1911–17 Studied painting and sculpture at the Hochschule für Bildende Kunst in Weimar. 1920 Study trip to France. 1924 Enrolment at the Staatliche Bauhaus Weimar, preliminary course under Josef Albers and László Moholy-Nagy, tuition with Paul Klee and Wassily Kandinsky. 1924–28 Metal workshops with László Moholy-Nagy in Weimar and Dessau. Head of lighting innovation, creating numerous lighting designs for the Bauhaus buildings in Dessau, some in collaboration with Hin Bredendieck. 1928–1929 Head of the metal workshop at the Bauhaus in Dessau, Bauhaus diploma. Production of numerous photographs and collages. 1929–30 Colleague in Gropius' Berlin office, 1930–33 Work in the Ruppelwerke metalwork factory in Gotha. Unemployed from 1933. 1949–51 Lecturer at the Hochschule fur Bildende Künste in Dresden, 1951–54 at the Hochschule für angewandte Kunst in Berlin-Weißensee. 1954 Retirement. Died 1983 in Kirchberg, Saxony.

Marcel Breuer (1902–1981) Architekt, Designer, 1902 in Pécs/Ungarn geboren. 1920 Immatrikulation am Staatlichen Bauhaus Weimar, Vorkurs bei Johannes Itten. 1920–24 Tischlerlehre bei Walter Gropius, Gesellenprüfung vor der Handwerkskammer Weimar. 1924/25 Geselle in der Tischlereiwerkstatt des Bauhauses. Aufenthalt in Paris. 1925–28 Jung-

meister der Tischlerei am Bauhaus Dessau, Entwurf des Klubsessels B3 als erstem Stahlrohrstuhl für den Wohnbedarf sowie zahlreicher Möbel für die Bauhausbauten in Dessau. 1928–33 Architekt und Designer in Berlin, 1933 Verlegung des Büros nach Budapest. 1935–37 Emigration nach England, Architekturbüro in London. 1937 Berufung als Professor für Architektur an die Graduate School of Design an der Harvard University in Cambridge, Massachusetts/USA. Bis 1941 in Cambridge gemeinsames Büro mit Walter Gropius, 1946 eigenes Büro in New York. 1956 Gründung von Marcel Breuer and Associates. Zahlreiche Aufträge für Privathäuser und ihre Einrichtung, Verwaltungs- und Universitätsgebäude sowie öffentliche Gebäude, u. a. das UNESCO-Gebäude in Paris und das Whitney Museum in New York. 1981 in New York gestorben.

Marcel Breuer (1902–1981) Architect, designer, Born 1902 in Pécs, Hungary. 1920 Enrolment at the Staatliche Bauhaus Weimar, preliminary course under Johannes Itten. 1920–24 Carpentry apprenticeship under Walter Gropius, journeyman's certificate from the chamber of trade in Weimar. 1924/25 Assistant in the Bauhaus carpentry workshop. Residence in Paris. 1925–28 Junior Master of the carpentry workshop at the Bauhaus in Dessau, design of the Club Chair B3, the first tubular steel chair designed as a household article, as well as numerous pieces of furniture for the Bauhaus buildings in Dessau. 1928–33 Architect and designer in Berlin. 1933 Transfer of office to Budapest. 1935–37 Emigration to England, architectural office in London. 1937 Appointment as Professor of Architecture at the Graduate School of Design of Harvard University in Cambridge, Massachusetts, USA. Until 1941 Joint office with Walter Gropius in Cambridge. 1946 Own office in New York. 1956 Foundation of Marcel Breuer and Associates. Numerous construction and interior design commissions for private, administrative, university and public buildings, incl. the UNESCO building in Paris and the Whitney Museum in New York. Died 1981 in New York.

Edmund Collein (1906–1992) Architekt, Stadtplaner, Fotograf, 1906 in Bad Kreuznach geboren. 1925–27 Architekturstudium an der TH Darmstadt. 1927 Immatrikulation am Bauhaus Dessau, Vorkurs bei László Moholy-Nagy, Unterricht bei Paul Klee, Wassily Kandinsky und Joost Schmidt. 1927–28 Tischlereiwerkstatt bei Marcel Breuer, 1928–30 Bau-/Ausbauabteilung bei Hannes Meyer, 1930 Bauhausdiplom. Bis 1940 Tätigkeit in Architekturbüros, dann Kriegsdienst und Gefangenschaft. 1945 Rückkehr nach Berlin, Arbeit beim Berliner Magistrat. 1950 Mitautor der „16 Grundsätze des Städtebaus der DDR". 1950er und 1960er Jahre Umsetzung der baupolitischen Richtlinien der SED für Magdeburg und Berlin. Am Bau der Berliner Karl-Marx-Allee beteiligt, zahlreiche öffentliche Ämter. 1992 in Berlin gestorben.

Edmund Collein (1906–1992) Architect, town planner, photographer, Born 1906 in Bad Kreuznach. 1925–27 Studied architecture at TH Darmstadt. 1927 Enrolment at the Bauhaus in Dessau, preliminary course under László Moholy-Nagy, tuition with Paul Klee, Wassily Kandinsky and Joost Schmidt. 1927–28 Carpentry workshop under Marcel Breuer. 1928–30 Construction department under Hannes Meyer. 1930 Bauhaus diploma. Until 1940 Work in architectural offices, then military service and imprisonment. 1945 Return to Berlin, work for the municipal authorities in Berlin. 1950 Co-author of the paper "16 Grundsätze des Städtebaus der DDR" (16 principles of urban development in the GDR). 1950s and 1960s Implementation of the building policies of the United Socialist Party in Magdeburg und Berlin. Participation in the construction of Karl-Marx-Allee in Berlin, numerous public commissions. Died 1992 in Berlin.

Erich Consemüller (1902–1957) Fotograf, Architekt, Stadtplaner, 1902 in Bielefeld geboren. Tischlerlehre, Besuch der Kunstgewerbeschule Bielefeld. 1922 Immatrikulation am Staatlichen Bauhaus Weimar, Vorkurs bei Johannes Itten, Unterricht bei Paul Klee und Wassily Kandinsky. 1923–25 Tischlereiwerkstatt bei Walter Gropius, 1924 Gesellenprüfung vor der Handwerkskammer Weimar. 1925–28 Tischlereiwerkstatt am Bauhaus Dessau bei Marcel Breuer, Beteiligung an der Ausstattung des Theatercafés Dessau und der Wohnung Erwin Piscators in Berlin. 1927 im Auftrag von Walter Gropius fotografische Dokumentation des Bauhausgebäudes. 1927–29 Bauabteilung bei Hannes Meyer, Mitarbeit an der Bundesschule des Allgemeinen Deutschen Gewerkschaftsbundes (ADGB) in Bernau bei Berlin und Bauprojekten von Hans Wittwer in Halle. 1929 Bauhausdiplom der Bauabteilung. 1929–33 Lehrer der Architektur- und der Werbeabteilung der Burg Giebichenstein in Halle/Saale. 1933 seines Amtes enthoben, bis 1945 Architekt und Hochbautechniker in Halle, Erfurt und Leipzig. 1945 Amt des Stadtplaners in Halle. 1957 in Halle gestorben.

Erich Consemüller (1902–1957) Photographer, architect, town planner, Born 1902 in Bielefeld. Carpentry apprenticeship, attendance at the Kunstgewerbeschule Bielefeld. 1922 Enrolment at the Staatliches Bauhaus Weimar, preliminary course under Johannes Itten, tuition with Paul Klee and Wassily Kandinsky. 1923–25 Carpentry workshop with Walter Gropius, 1924 Journeyman's certificate from the chamber of trade in Weimar. 1925–28 Carpentry workshop at the Bauhaus in Dessau under Marcel Breuer, collaboration on the interior design of the Theatre café in Dessau and Erwin Piscator's apartment in Berlin. 1927 Photographic documentation of the Bauhaus Building for Walter Gropius. 1927–29 Department of Architecture with Hannes Meyer. Collaboration on the Bundesschule des Allgemeinen Deutschen Gewerkschaftsbundes (ADGB) in Bernau near Berlin and construction projects led by Hans Wittwer in Halle. 1929 Bauhaus diploma awarded by the department of architecture. 1929–33 Professor in the department of architecture and advertising at Burg Giebichenstein in Halle/Saale. 1933 Dismissed from his post. Architect and structural engineer in Halle, Erfurt and Leipzig to 1945. 1945 Post as town planner in Halle. Died 1957 in Halle.

Franz Ehrlich (1907–1984) Architekt, Stadtplaner, Designer, 1907 in Leipzig geboren. Ausbildung zum Maschinenschlosser, bis 1926 Maschinist und Heizer. 1927 Immatrikulation am Bauhaus Dessau, Vorkurs bei László Moholy-Nagy, Unterricht bei Paul Klee, Wassily Kandinsky und Joost Schmidt. 1927–1930 Plastische Werkstatt bei Joost Schmidt, Bauhausdiplom. 1930 Gesellenprüfung als Tischler. Übersiedlung nach Berlin, mit den Bauhäuslern Heinz Loew und Fritz Winter Gründung des Werbebüros Studio Z. 1934 Verhaftung wegen seines kommunistischen Engagements. Konzentrationslager, Arbeitsdienst, Strafbataillon und Kriegsgefangenschaft. Ab 1946 Architekt und Stadtplaner in Dresden. 1950 Berufung zum technischen Direktor des Entwurfsbüros für Industriebau der DDR in Berlin. Ab 1955 Architekt des Ministeriums für Außenwirtschaft der DDR, Beteiligung am Bau sowie der Innenausstattung zahlreicher ausländischer Handelsvertretungen, u. a. in Brüssel. Mit Gerhard Probst Bau des Rundfunkzentrums in Berlin-Adlershof. 1963–66 Chefarchitekt der Leipziger Messe, ab 1968 Hausarchitekt der Deutschen Werkstätten in Dresden-Hellerau, Entwicklung von Möbel-Typenbausätzen. 1984 in Bernburg gestorben.

Franz Ehrlich (1907–1984) Architect, town planner, designer, Born 1907 in Leipzig. Trained as a machine fitter. Work as a machine operator and boiler man until 1926. 1927 Enrolment at the Bauhaus in Dessau, preliminary course with László Moholy-Nagy, tuition with Paul Klee, Wassily Kandinsky and Joost Schmidt. 1927–1930 Sculpture workshop under Joost Schmidt, Bauhaus diploma. 1930 Journeyman's certificate as a carpenter, relocation to Berlin, foundation of the Studio Z advertising bureau with Bauhaus associates Heinz Loew and Fritz Winter. 1934 Arrest due to communist activities. Concentration camp, labour service, penal battalion and war captivity. From 1946 Architect und town planner in Dresden. 1950 Appointment in Berlin as technical director of the design office for industrial architecture in the GDR. From 1955 Architect in the GDR's ministry for foreign trade, participation in the construction and interior design of numerous foreign trade missions in, for example, Brussels. Collaboration with Gerhard Probst on the construction of the broadcasting centre in Berlin-Adlershof. 1963–66 Chief architect of the Leipzig trade fair, from 1968 interoffice architect of the Deutsche Werkstätten in Dresden-Hellerau, development of prototype furniture construction kits. Died 1984 in Bernburg.

Lyonel Feininger (1871–1956) Maler, 1871 in New York geboren. 1887 Studium an der Hamburger Gewerbeschule und der Kunstakademie Berlin, 1909 Mitglied der Berliner Sezession. 1919 Mitglied im Arbeitsrat für Kunst, als erster Meister von Gropius ans Staatliche Bauhaus Weimar berufen. Sein Holzschnitt „Kathedrale" wird Titel des Bauhaus-Manifestes. 1921–25 Formmeister der Grafischen Druckerei. 1926–32 Meister ohne Lehrverpflichtung am Bauhaus Dessau, ab 1924 Mitglied der Künstlergruppe „Die blauen Vier". Zahlreiche Ausstellungen im In- und Ausland.

1933 Übersiedlung nach Berlin. 1937 Rückkehr nach New York, erfolgreiche Arbeit als Maler. 1944 Retrospektive im Museum of Modern Art in New York. 1947 Präsident der "Federation of American Painters and Sculptors". Dozent am Mills College in Oakland, Kalifornien und am Black Mountain College in Ashville, North Carolina. 1956 in New York gestorben.

Lyonel Feininger (1871–1956) Painter, Born 1871 in New York. 1887 Studied at the Gewerbeschule in Hamburg and the Kunstakademie in Berlin. 1909 Member of the German artists' association Berliner Sezession. 1919 Member of the association of radical architects, artists and critics Arbeitsrat für Kunst, appointed by Gropius as the first Master of the Staatliches Bauhaus Weimar. His "Cathedral" woodcut appears on the cover of the Bauhaus manifesto. 1921–25 Form Master in the graphics section of the printing workshop. 1926–32 Master (without teaching duties) at the Bauhaus in Dessau, from 1924 member of the artists' group "Die blauen Vier". Numerous exhibitions at home and abroad. 1933 Relocation to Berlin. 1937 Return to New York, success as a painter. 1944 Retrospective in the Museum of Modern Art in New York. 1947 President of the Federation of American Painters and Sculptors. Lecturer at Mills College in Oakland, California and Black Mountain College in Ashville, North Carolina. Died 1956 in New York.

Carl Fieger (1893–1960) Architekt, 1893 in Mainz geboren. Studium an der dortigen Kunst- und Gewerbeschule, ab 1911 Zeichner bei Peter Behrens in Berlin, ab 1912–34 mit Unterbrechungen Mitarbeiter im Büro von Walter Gropius in Berlin, Weimar und Dessau. 1921 nebenamtlicher Lehrer für Architekturzeichnen am Staatlichen Bauhaus Weimar. 1926 eigenes Büro in Dessau, Entwurf seines eigenen Wohnhauses als Modell eines Kleinhauses. 1927–30 nebenamtlicher Lehrer für Fachzeichnen und darstellende Geometrie am Bauhaus Dessau. 1928 Übersiedlung nach Berlin. 1930 Bau des Restaurants Kornhaus in Dessau. 1934 Berufsverbot. 1945–47 Bestrebungen zur Wiedereröffnung des Bauhauses, Planungen für den Wiederaufbau von Dessau. 1952 Berufung an die Deutschen Bauakademie (DDR) durch Richard Paulick. 1960 in Dessau gestorben.

Carl Fieger (1893–1960) Architect, Born 1893 in Mainz. Studied at the Kunst- und Gewerbeschule in Mainz. From 1911 Draughtsman in Peter Behrens' office in Berlin. From 1912–34 Part-time work in Walter Gropius' offices in Berlin, Weimar and Dessau. 1921 Part-time tutor in architectural draughtsmanship at the Staatliches Bauhaus Weimar. 1926 Own office in Dessau, design of his own house as a prototype of a small residential dwelling. 1927–30 Part-time tutor in specialized draughtsmanship and illustrative geometry at the Bauhaus in Dessau. 1928 Relocation to Berlin. 1930 Construction of the Kornhaus restaurant in Dessau. 1934 Employment ban. 1945–47 Attempts to re-open the Bauhaus, designs for the post-war reconstruction of Dessau. 1952 Nominated as a member of the Deutsche Bauakademie (GDR) by Richard Paulick. Died 1960 in Dessau

Walter Gropius (1883–1969) Architekt, 1883 in Berlin geboren. 1903–07 Studium der Architektur in Berlin und München. 1908–10 Mitarbeiter verschiedener Büros in München und Berlin, u. a. bei Peter Behrens. Eigenes Architekturbüro. 1911 Mitglied des Deutschen Werkbundes, Bau der Fagus-Werke in Alfeld an der Leine mit Adolf Meyer. 1918–19 Mitglied des Arbeitsrates für Kunst. 1919–28 Direktor des Staatlichen Bauhauses Weimar und des Bauhauses Dessau. 1922–25 Formmeister der Tischlerei in Weimar. Ab 1925 in Dessau Entwurf des Bauhausgebäudes, der Meisterhäuser, der Siedlung Törten mit dem Konsumgebäude sowie des Arbeitsamtes. 1928 Rückzug vom Bauhaus, Gründungsmitglied des CIAM (Congrès International d'Architecture Moderne). 1928–34 freier Architekt in Berlin, Entwurf u. a. der Siedlungen Karlsruhe-Dammerstock und Berlin-Siemensstadt. 1934 Emigration nach London, bis 1937 Büro mit Maxwell Fry. 1937 Berufung an die Graduate School of Design der Harvard University in Cambridge, Massachusetts/USA. Ab 1938 Leiter der Architekturabteilung, Organisation der Ausstellung „Bauhaus 1919–1928" im Museum of Modern Art in New York. Bis 1941 gemeinsames Architekturbüro mit Marcel Breuer, Bau zahlreicher Villen in den USA. 1946 Gründung des Büros The Architects Collaborative (TAC), Bau u. a. des Harvard University Graduate Center. Beteiligung unter anderem 1957 an der Interbau Berlin und ab 1961 am Bau der Siedlung Buckow-Britz in Berlin, Entwurf für das Bauhaus-Archiv. 1969 in Boston gestorben.

Walter Gropius (1883–1969) Architect, Born 1883 in Berlin. 1903–07 Studied architecture in Berlin and Munich. 1908–10 Employee in a number of offices in Munich and Berlin, e.g., with Peter Behrens. Own architectural office. 1911 Member of the Deutscher Werkbund. Construction, in collaboration with Adolf Meyer, of the Fagus-Werke factory in Alfeld an der Leine. 1918–19 Member of the association of radical architects, artists and critics Arbeitsrat für Kunst. 1919–28 Director of the Staatliches Bauhaus Weimar and the Bauhaus in Dessau. 1922–25 Form Master of the carpentry workshop in Weimar. From 1925 In Dessau, design of the Bauhaus Building, the Masters' Houses, the Törten Estate incl. the Konsum Building, and the Employment Office. 1928 Retreat from the Bauhaus, founding member of CIAM (Congrès International d'Architecture Moderne). 1928–34 Freelance architect in Berlin. Design of, among others, the Karlsruhe-Dammerstock Estate and the Berlin-Siemensstadt Estate. 1934 Emigration to London. Until 1937 Joint office with Maxwell Fry. 1937 Appointment at the Graduate School of Design Harvard University in Cambridge, Massachusetts, USA. From 1938 Head of the Department of Architecture, organisation of the exhibition "Bauhaus 1919–1928" in the Museum of Modern Art in New York. To 1941 Joint architectural office with Marcel Breuer, construction of numerous villas in the USA. 1946 Foundation of The Architects Collaborative (TAC), construction of, among others, the Harvard University Graduate Center. Participation in, among other things, the exhibition Interbau Berlin in 1957, the construction of the Buckow-Britz Estate in Berlin from 1961, and the development of the Bauhaus Archive. Died 1969 in Boston.

Ludwig Grote (1893–1974) Kunsthistoriker, 1893 in Halle/Saale geboren. 1912–19 Studium der Archäologie und Architektur in Jena und Braunschweig, 1919–22 Studium der Kunstgeschichte in Halle, 1922 Promotion. 1924–33 Landeskonservator von Anhalt, persönlicher Berater des Dessauer Bürgermeisters Fritz Hesse. Maßgebliche Beteiligung an der Übersiedlung des Bauhauses nach Dessau, Verhandlungsführer der Gespräche mit Walter Gropius. Einrichtung seiner Wohnung mit Möbeln von Marcel Breuer. Ab 1927 nebenamtlich Direktor der von ihm gegründeten Gemäldegalerie in Dessau (Palais Reina), Übertragung der farbigen Ausgestaltung an Hinnerk Scheper. 1933 u. a. wegen des Ankaufs von Bildern von Bauhausmalern des Amtes enthoben. Ab 1933 freiberufliche Tätigkeit. Nach 1945 Organisation zahlreicher Ausstellungen in München, z. B. 1950 „Die Maler am Bauhaus". Ab 1951 Direktor des Germanischen Nationalmuseums in Nürnberg. 1974 in Gauting bei München gestorben.

Ludwig Grote (1893–1974) Art historian, Born 1893 in Halle/Saale. 1912–19 Studied archaeology and architecture in Jena and Braunschweig. 1919–22 Studied art history in Halle, 1922 Doctorate. 1924–33 State conservation officer in Anhalt, personal advisor to the Lord Mayor, Fritz Hesse. Significant advocate of the Bauhaus' relocation to Dessau, leading negotiations with Walter Gropius. Furnishes his residence with furniture by Marcel Breuer. From 1927 Founder and part-time director of the Palais Reina picture gallery in Dessau, commissioning Hinnerk Scheper with its interior colour design. 1933 Dismissed from his post for, among other things, the purchase of pictures by Bauhaus painters. Freelance from 1933. From 1945 Organisation of numerous exhibitions in Munich, e.g., „Die Maler am Bauhaus" in 1950. From 1951 Director of the Germanisches Nationalmuseum in Nuremberg. Died 1974 in Gauting near Munich.

Fritz Hesse (1881–1973) Jurist, Politiker, 1881 in Dessau geboren. Studium der Rechtswissenschaften in Jena, Berlin und Halle/Saale. 1907 Niederlassung als Rechtsanwalt in Dessau, 1911 Wahl zum Stadtverordneten. 1918 Mitbegründer der Deutschen Demokratischen Partei (DDP). 1920–24 Landtagsabgeordneter in Anhalt, ab 1918 Bürgermeister von Dessau. 1925 maßgebliche Initiative für die Übersiedlung des Bauhauses nach Dessau. Ab 1929 Oberbürgermeister von Dessau. 1933 von der NSDAP des Amtes enthoben, danach Anwalt in Berlin. 1945–46 erneut Bürgermeister von Dessau, vergebliche Bemühungen um eine Wiederbelebung des Bauhauses. Mit Gründung der SED abgesetzt. Ab 1946 Rechtsanwalt in Dessau, Berlin und München. 1973 in Bad Neuenahr gestorben.

Fritz Hesse (1881–1973) Lawyer, politician, Born 1881 in Dessau. Studied law in Jena, Berlin and Halle/Saale. 1907 Lawyer in Dessau. 1911 Election as town councillor. 1918 Co-founder of the German Democratic Party. 1920–24 Member of the Landtag legislative assembly in Anhalt, from 1918 Mayor of Dessau. 1925 Active in the initiative to bring the Bauhaus to Dessau. From 1929 Lord Mayor of Dessau. 1933 Removed from his post by the NSDAP, later lawyer in Berlin. 1945–46 Again Mayor of Dessau, failed attempts to re-open the Bauhaus. Deposed with the foundation of the United Socialist Party. From 1946 Lawyer in Dessau, Berlin and Munich. Died 1973 in Bad Neuenahr.

Ludwig Hilberseimer (1885–1967) Architekt, Stadtplaner, 1885 in Karlsruhe geboren. Studium der Architektur, Geschichte, Philosophie und Literatur. 1915 Angestellter bei einer Fliegerversuchs- und Lehranstalt, später Leiter von deren Architekturbüro. Nach 1918 Tätigkeit als Kunstkritiker. Ab 1922 erste Bauprojekte in Berlin, Wohnhäuser und Siedlungen. 1926 Mitbegründer der Architektenvereinigung „Der Ring". 1927 Vorstandsmitglied des Deutschen Werkbundes, Beteiligung am Bau der Weißenhofsiedlung in Stuttgart. Veröffentlichung der Publikationen „Großstadtarchitektur" 1927 und „Beton als Gestalter" 1928. 1929 Berufung ans Bauhaus Dessau, Lehrer für Konstruktives Entwerfen, Leitung der Baulehre, Lehrer für Wohnungs- und Städtebau. 1938 Emigration in die USA. Bis 1955 Professor für Stadt- und Regionalplanung am Illinois Institute of Technology in Chicago, danach Direktor der Abteilung. 1967 in Chicago gestorben.

Ludwig Hilberseimer (1885–1967) Architect, town planner, Born 1885 in Karlsruhe. Studied architecture, history, philosophy and literature. 1915 Employee at an aviation research and training institute, later head of their architectural office. From 1918 Work as an art critic. From 1922 First construction projects in Berlin, incl. residential houses and estates. 1926 Co-founder of the architectural collective "Der Ring". 1927 Board member of the Deutscher Werkbund, participation in the construction of the Weissenhof Estate in Stuttgart. Publication of the books "Großstadtarchitektur" in 1927 and "Beton als Gestalter" in 1928. 1929 Appointment at the Bauhaus in Dessau, tutor in structural design, also head of architectural theory and tutor in house construction and town planning. 1938 Emigration to the USA. To 1955 Professor for town and regional planning at the Illinois Institute of Technology in Chicago, later director of the department. Died 1967 in Chicago.

Johannes Itten (1888–1976) Maler, Kunstpädagoge, 1888 in Süderen-Linden/Schweiz geboren. Zunächst Volksschullehrer. 1913 Studium der Malerei bei Adolf Hölzel in Stuttgart. 1916 Ausstellung in der Berliner „Sturm"-Galerie, Gründung einer Kunstschule in Wien. 1919 Berufung ans Staatliche Bauhaus Weimar, Einrichtung des Vorkurses. 1920–1923 Formmeister der meisten Werkstätten. 1923 Übersiedlung in die Schweiz in eine Mazdaznan-Tempelgemeinschaft nahe Zürich. 1926 Gründung der Ittenschule Berlin, einer modernen Kunstschule. 1932–38 Direktor der Höheren Fachschule für textile Flächenkunst in Krefeld. 1934 Schließung der Ittenschule Berlin durch die Nationalsozialisten. 1938–53 Direktor der Kunstgewerbeschule und des Kunstgewerbemuseums in Zürich. 1950–56 Aufbau und Leitung des Rietberg-Museums für außereuropäische Kunst in Zürich, 1976 dort gestorben.

Johannes Itten (1888–1976) Painter, art teacher, Born 1888 in Süderen-Linden, Switzerland. Elementary school teacher. 1913 Studied painting under Adolf Hölzel in Stuttgart. 1916 Exhibition in the "Der Sturm" gallery in Berlin, foundation of an art school in Vienna. 1919 Appointment at the Staatliches Bauhaus Weimar, establishing the preliminary course. 1920–1923 Form Master in most of the workshops. 1923 Relocation to Mazdaznan temple community near Zurich, Switzerland. 1926 Foundation of a modern art school, the Ittenschule, in Berlin. 1932–38 Director of the Höhere Fachschule für textile Flächenkunst in Krefeld. 1934 Closure of the Ittenschule by the National Socialists. 1938–53 Director of the Kunstgewerbeschule and the Kunstgewerbemuseum in Zurich. 1950–56 Foundation and directorship of the Rietberg Museum for non-European art in Zurich. Died 1976 in Zurich.

Hugo Junkers (1859–1935) Ingenieur, Unternehmer, 1859 in Rheydt/Rheinland geboren. Studium der Ingenieurwissenschaften in Berlin, Karlsruhe und Aachen. 1895 Gründung der Firma Junkers & Co. in Dessau, die v. a. Wärmeaustauschapparate produziert, 1915 Gründung einer Forschungsanstalt für Flugzeugbau. 1919 Start des ersten zivilen Ganzmetallflugzeugs und Gründung der „Junkers-Flugzeugwerke AG" in Dessau. Ab 1925 vielfältige Kontakte zum Bauhaus, Mitglied im Kreis der Freunde, Beschäftigung von Studierenden der Metallwerkstatt. Verwendung von Junkers-Produkten wie Wärmetechnik, Serienheizkörper, Thermen in den Bauhausbauten. Ausführung der gekuppelten Drehfenster durch Junkers-Stahlbau. Ausstattung u. a. des 1928 eröffneten Verwaltungsgebäudes von Junkers in Dessau mit Bauhaus-Leuchten. Entwurf von Broschüren und Ausstellungsgestaltungen für die Firma Junkers durch die Werkstatt für Typografie des Bauhauses. Bau eines Lamellen-Stahlhauses, Beschäftigung mit dem standardisierten Metallhausbau. 1930 Entwurf einer Junkers-Siedlung durch die Bauabteilung des Bauhauses. 1933 Zwangsübereignung der Junkers-Patente an den nationalsozialistischen Staat, Hausarrest. 1935 in Gauting bei München gestorben.

Hugo Junkers (1859–1935) Engineer, businessman, Born 1859 in Rheydt, Rhineland. Studied engineering in Berlin, Karlsruhe and Aachen. 1895 Foundation of Junkers & Co. in Dessau, manufacturing, e.g., heat exchange devices. 1915 Foundation of a research institute for aircraft construction. 1919 Launch of the first civil all-metal aircraft and foundation of Junkers-Flugzeugwerke AG in Dessau. From 1925 Varied contacts to the Bauhaus, member of Friends of the Bauhaus, employment of students from the metal workshop. Use of Junkers products such as heating technology, series radiators and boilers in the Bauhaus buildings. Manufac-

ture of vaulted rotating windows by Junkers-Stahlbau. 1928 Fitting of Bauhaus lighting in, for example, the Junkers administration building. Design of brochures and exhibitions for Junkers in the Bauhaus typography workshop. Construction of a rib steel building, pursuit of standardised metal house construction. 1930 Development of the Junkers Estate with the Bauhaus department of architecture. 1933 Compulsory transfer of Junkers patents to the National Socialist state, house arrest. Died 1935 in Gauting near Munich.

Wassily Kandinsky (1866–1944) Maler, 1866 in Moskau geboren. Studium der Rechtswissenschaften, Arbeit als Jurist. 1896 Übersiedlung nach München. Studium bei Franz von Stuck und Mitgründung der Künstlergruppe „Phalanx". 1908 Bekanntschaft mit Gabriele Münter, Entstehung der Murnau-Bilder beider Künstler. 1911 erscheint „Über das Geistige in der Kunst". Gründung der Künstlergemeinschaft „Blauer Reiter" mit Franz Marc, erste abstrakte Bilder. 1914 Flucht aus Deutschland. In Moskau Entwicklung von Programmen für das Institut für künstlerische Kultur, Lehrer an den Höheren künstlerischen und technischen Werkstätten. 1922 Berufung ans Staatliche Bauhaus Weimar, bis 1925 Formmeister der Wandmalereiwerkstatt. Lehrer für Analytisches Zeichnen und Abstrakte Formelemente. Ab 1924 Mitglied der Künstlergruppe „Die blauen Vier". 1926 erscheint „Punkt und Linie zu Fläche". 1926–1933 Leiter der freien Malklasse. 1932–33 Bauhaus Berlin, Lehrer für Abstrakte Formelemente und Analytisches Zeichnen im Vorkurs. 1933 Emigration nach Paris. 1944 in Neuilly sur Seine bei Paris gestorben.

Wassily Kandinsky (1866–1944) Painter, Born 1866 in Moscow. Studied law, worked as a lawyer. 1896 Relocation to Munich. Studied art under Franz von Stuck, co-founder of the art group "Phalanx". 1908 Companionship with Gabriele Münter, creation of the Murnau pictures by both artists. 1911 Publication of "Über das Geistige in der Kunst" (Concerning the Spiritual in Art). Foundation of the art group "Der Blaue Reiter" with Franz Marc, first abstract paintings. 1914 Flight from Germany. Development of programmes for the Moscow institute for artistic culture, tutor in fine art and technical workshops. 1922 Appointment at the Staatliches Bauhaus Weimar. To 1925 Form Master in the wall painting workshop. Tutor in analytical drawing and abstract forms. From 1924 Member of the art group "Die blauen Vier". 1926 Publication of "Punkt und Linie zu Fläche" (Point and Line to Plane). 1926–1933 Head of free painting. 1932–33 At the Bauhaus in Berlin, preliminary course tutor in abstract form elements and analytical drawing. 1933 Emigration to Paris. Died 1944 in Neuilly sur Seine near Paris.

Paul Klee (1879–1940) Maler, 1879 in Münchenbuchsee/Schweiz geboren. 1898–1901 Studium bei Franz von Stuck in München, Ausstellung bei der Gruppe „Blauer Reiter". 1914 Reise nach Tunesien mit August Macke und Louis Moilliet, die Bilder der „Tunisreise" begründen seinen Ruf als wichtiger Expressionist. 1921 Berufung ans Staatliche Bauhaus Weimar, bis 1930 in Weimar und Dessau Unterricht Elementare Gestaltungslehre im Vorkurs. Ab 1921 Leitung der Buchbinderei, 1922 der Metallwerkstatt, 1922–25 der Glasmalereiwerkstatt. 1924 Mitglied der Künstlergruppe „Die blauen Vier". 1925 erscheint das „Pädagogische Skizzenbuch". 1926–30 Unterricht freie plastische und malerische Gestaltung, ab 1927 freie Malklasse. 1927–30 auf Wunsch der Weberinnen Unterricht Gestaltungslehre in der Textilwerkstatt. 1931 Berufung an die Kunstakademie Düsseldorf, 1933 Entlassung durch die Nationalsozialisten. Emigration in die Schweiz. 1940 in Muralto/Schweiz gestorben.

Paul Klee (1879–1940) Painter, Born 1879 in Münchenbuchsee, Switzerland. 1898–1901 Studied art under Franz von Stuck in Munich, exhibition with the art group "Der Blaue Reiter". 1914 Trip to Tunisia with August Macke and Louis Moilliet. The "Tunisian Journey" paintings establish his reputation as an important Expressionist. 1921 Appointment at the Staatliches Bauhaus Weimar. To 1930 Tutor in elementary design in the preliminary courses in Weimar and Dessau. From 1921 Head of bookbinding, 1922 head of the metal workshop, 1922–25 head of the glass-painting workshop. 1924 Member of the art group "Die blauen Vier". 1925 Publication of the "Pädagogisches Skizzenbuch" (Pedagogical sketchbook). 1926–30 Tutor in free sculptural and painting design and, from 1927, free painting. 1927–30 Requested by weavers to teach design in the textile workshop. 1931 Appointment at the Kunstakademie Düsseldorf. 1933 Removed from his post by the National Socialists. Emigration to Switzerland. Died 1940 in Muralto, Switzerland.

Max Krajewski (1901–1971) Metalldesigner, 1901 in Polen geboren. Lehre als Metalldreher. 1919 Übersiedlung nach Deutschland, Arbeit im Ruhrgebiet u. a. im Bergbau. 1923 Immatrikulation am Staatlichen Bauhaus Weimar, Vorkurs bei László Moholy-Nagy, Unterricht bei Wassily Kandinsky und Paul Klee. 1924–27 Metallwerkstatt in Weimar und Dessau, 1925 Fertigung von Möbeln und Leuchten für das Bauhausgebäude. 1927 Studienabschluss. Tätigkeit im Baubüro Gropius, Bauleiter der Siedlung Dessau-Törten und des Arbeitsamtes Dessau. 1929 Bauleiter der Siedlung Karlsruhe-Dammerstock. 1931 Übersiedlung nach Moskau, Arbeit als Architekt. 1971 in Moskau gestorben.

Max Krajewski (1901–1971) Metal designer, Born 1901 in Poland. Apprenticeship as a metal turner. 1919 Relocation to Germany. Work, incl. mining, in the Ruhr Area. 1923 Enrolment at the Staatliches Bauhaus Weimar, preliminary course under László Moholy-Nagy, tuition with Wassily Kandinsky and Paul Klee. 1924–27 Metal workshop in Weimar and Dessau, 1925 production of furniture and lighting for the Bauhaus Building. 1927 Final diploma. Work in Gropius' architectural office, construction supervisor of the Dessau-Törten Estate and the Employment Office in Dessau. 1929 Head of construction at the Karlsruhe-Dammerstock

Estate. 1931 Relocation to Moscow, work as an architect. Died 1971 in Moscow.

Hannes Meyer (1889–1954) Architekt, Stadtplaner, 1889 in Basel/Schweiz geboren. Studium an der Gewerbeschule Basel, Maurerlehrling, Bauzeichner und Bauführer. 1916 Bürochef in einem Münchner Architekturbüro. Bis 1918 Ressortchef bei der Kruppschen Bauverwaltung in Essen. 1919 freier Architekt, u. a. Bau der Siedlung Freidorf bei Basel. Bis 1927 Mitarbeiter bei Hans Wittwer, Entwürfe für die Petersschule in Basel und das Völkerbundgebäude in Genf. 1927 Berufung als Leiter der Bauabteilung an das Bauhaus Dessau. 1928–30 Direktor des Bauhauses. Ausbau der Werkstätten zu Produktions- und Forschungszellen. 1929–30 gemeinsam mit der Bauabteilung Entwurf der Laubenganghäuser in Dessau, 1928–30 der Bundesschule des Allgemeinen Deutschen Gewerkschaftsbundes (ADGB) in Bernau bei Berlin. 1930 fristlose Entlassung, mit zahlreichen Bauhaus-Studierenden Übersiedlung nach Moskau. Professor an der Architekturhochschule. 1934 Professor und Leiter des Kabinetts für Wohnungswesen an der Architektur-Akademie in Moskau. 1936 Rückkehr in die Schweiz, 1939 Direktor des Instituts für Stadtbau und Planung in Mexiko, zahlreiche öffentliche Ämter, 1949 Rückkehr in die Schweiz. 1954 in Crossifisso di Lugano/Schweiz gestorben.

Hannes Meyer (1889–1954) Architect, town planner, Born 1889 in Basel, Switzerland. Studied at the Gewerbeschule Basel, apprenticeship as a bricklayer, architectural draughtsman and construction supervisor. 1916 Head clerk of an architectural office in Munich. Until 1918 Construction manager for Krupp in Essen. 1919 Freelance architect. Construction of, among others, the Freidorf Estate near Basel. To 1927 Employee in Hans Wittwer's office, designs for the Petersschule in Basel and the League of Nations building in Geneva. 1927 Appointment as head of the department of architecture at the Bauhaus in Dessau. 1928–30 Director of the Bauhaus. Development of the workshops as centres of production and research. 1929–30 Collaboration with the department of architecture on, among others, the design of the Balcony Access Houses in Dessau and 1928–30 the Bundesschule des Allgemeinen Deutschen Gewerkschaftsbundes (ADGB) in Bernau near Berlin. 1930 Summary dismissal, relocation to Moscow along with many other Bauhaus students, professor at the Moscow school of architecture. 1934 Professor and head of the housing department at the academy of architecture in Moscow. 1936 Return to Switzerland. 1939 Director of the institute for urban development and planning in Mexico, assumption of a number of public posts. 1949 Return to Switzerland. Died 1954 in Crossifisso di Lugano, Switzerland.

Ludwig Mies van der Rohe (1886–1969) Architekt, 1886 als Ludwig Mies in Aachen geboren. Mit dem Nachnamen seiner Mutter Agnes Rohe später Bildung seines Künstlernamens. 1899–1905 Maurerlehre,

Lehre als Stuck- und Ornamentzeichner. 1908–11 Arbeit im Büro von Peter Behrens, Bekanntschaft mit Gropius und Le Corbusier. 1919 eigenes Büro in Berlin. 1921 Mitglied der Novembergruppe, Entwurf eines Glashochhauses für die Berliner Friedrichstraße. 1925 künstlerischer Leiter des Deutschen Werkbundes, Denkmal für Rosa Luxemburg und Karl Liebknecht. 1926 Mitbegründer der Architektenvereinigung „Der Ring". 1926–27 Organisation der Werkbundausstellung „Die Wohnung" in Stuttgart-Weißenhof. 1929 Entwurf des „Barcelona-Pavillons" zur Weltausstellung. 1930–33 Direktor des Bauhauses in Dessau und Berlin, Leiter der Baulehre. Ausrichtung der Schule auf die Architekturausbildung. Nach 1933 freier Architekt, Ausstellungsgestaltungen. 1937 Emigration in die USA. 1938–58 Leiter des Armour Institute, später Illinois Institute of Technology in Chicago. Bauten u. a.: 1946–51 Farnsworth House in Illinois, 1950–51 Apartmenthäuser am Lake Shore Drive in Chicago, 1954–58 Seagram Building in New York, 1965–68 Neue Nationalgalerie in Berlin. 1969 in Chicago gestorben.

Ludwig Mies van der Rohe (1886–1969) Architect, Born Ludwig Mies 1886 in Aachen. Later used his mother's maiden name, Agnes Rohe, to form his alias. 1899–1905 Apprenticeship as a bricklayer, further training as a draughtsman of stucco ornaments. 1908–11 Employed in Peter Behrens' office, acquaintanceship with Gropius and Le Corbusier. 1919 Own office in Berlin. 1921 Member of the November Group, design of the glass Friedrichstrasse skyscraper in Berlin. 1925 Artistic head of the Deutscher Werkbund, monument for Rosa Luxemburg and Karl Liebknecht. 1926 Co-founder of the architectural collective "Der Ring". 1926–27 Organisation of the Werkbund's housing exhibition "Die Wohnung" in Stuttgart-Weissenhof. 1929 Design of the German Pavilion for the Barcelona World Fair. 1930–33 Director of the Bauhaus in Dessau and Berlin, head of architectural theory, realignment of the school's educational policy in favour of architecture. From 1933 Freelance architect, exhibition designer. 1937 Emigration to the USA. 1938–58 Head of the Armour Institute, later Illinois Institute of Technology, in Chicago. Designed, among others, 1946–51 Farnsworth House in Illinois, 1950–51 Lake Shore Drive Apartments in Chicago, 1954–58 Seagram Building in New York, 1965–68 Neue Nationalgalerie in Berlin. Died 1969 in Chicago.

Lucia Moholy, geb. Schulz (1894–1989) Fotografin, Publizistin, 1894 in Prag geboren. 1912–14 Studium der Philosophie, Philologie und Kunstgeschichte. 1914–23 Tätigkeit bei verschiedenen Verlagen in Wiesbaden und Leipzig. 1923 Fotografenlehre, Fotografieunterricht an der Kunstgewerbeschule Leipzig. 1923/24 fotografische Dokumentation der Bauhaus-Produkte, 1925–26 der Bauhausbauten. Redaktionelle Mitarbeit an vielen Bauhaus-Büchern. 1928 Übersiedlung nach Berlin, Bühnenfotografin. 1929–31 Dozentin für Fotografie an der Ittenschule in Berlin. 1933 Flucht über Prag, Wien und Frankreich nach London, 1959 Übersiedlung in die Schweiz. International renommierte Fotografin, Kritikerin des Bauhauses und Publizistin von Schriften zur Kulturgeschichte der Fotografie. 1989 in der Nähe von Zürich gestorben.

Lucia Moholy, born Schulz (1894–1989) Photographer, publicist, Born 1894 in Prague. 1912–14 Studied philosophy, philology and art history. 1914–23 Work in a number of publishing houses in Wiesbaden and Leipzig. 1923 Apprenticeship in photography, photography course at the Kunstgewerbeschule Leipzig. 1923/24 Photographic documentation of Bauhaus products and 1925/26 of the Bauhaus buildings. Co-editor of many Bauhaus books. 1928 Relocation to Berlin, stage photographer. 1929–31 Lecturer in photography at the Ittenschule in Berlin. 1933 Emigration via Prague, Vienna and France to London. 1959 Relocation to Switzerland. Internationally acclaimed photographer, Bauhaus critic and writer on the cultural history of photography. Died 1989 near Zurich.

László Moholy-Nagy (1895–1946) Fotograf, Maler, Grafikdesigner, 1895 in Bácsborsód/Ungarn geboren. Studium der Rechtswissenschaften in Budapest, an Kunstschulen in Szeged und Budapest. 1920 Übersiedlung nach Berlin. Kontakte zu Dadaisten und zur Galerie „Der Sturm", dort 1922 erste Einzelausstellung. Teilnahme am ersten Konstruktivisten-Kongress in Weimar. 1923 Berufung ans Staatliche Bauhaus Weimar, Beschäftigung mit Typografie und experimentellem Film. 1923–28 in Weimar und Dessau Leiter des Vorkurses und der Metallwerkstatt. Mit Walter Gropius Herausgabe der Bauhausbücher. 1928 Übersiedlung nach Berlin, Atelier für Typografie und Ausstellungsgestaltung. 1929 Bühnenbildner für die Kroll-Oper und die Piscator-Bühne. 1933 Emigration über Amsterdam nach London. 1937 Berufung nach Chicago, Illinois/USA, Gründung des New Bauhaus – American School of Design. 1939 Gründung seiner eigenen „School of Design", heute Teil des Illinois Institute of Technology (IIT). 1946 in Chicago gestorben.

László Moholy-Nagy (1895–1946) Photographer, painter, graphic designer, Born 1895 in Bácsborsód, Hungary. Studied law in Budapest and art at schools in Szeged and Budapest. 1920 Relocation to Berlin. Contact with the Dadaists and with the "Der Sturm" gallery. First exhibition there in 1922. Participation in the first constructivist congress in Weimar. 1923 Appointment at the Staatliches Bauhaus Weimar, pursuing typography and experimental filmmaking. 1923–28 Head of the preliminary courses and metal workshops in Weimar und Dessau. Publication, in collaboration with Walter Gropius, of the Bauhaus books. 1928 Relocation to Berlin, studio for typography and exhibition design. 1929 Stage designer for the Kroll-Oper opera house and the Piscator-Bühne theatre. 1933 Emigration via Amsterdam to London. 1937 Appointment to Chicago, Illinois, USA, and foundation of the New Bauhaus – American School of Design. 1939 Foundation of his own "School of Design", now part of the Illinois Institute of Technology (IIT). Died 1946 in Chicago.

Georg Muche (1895–1987) Maler, 1895 in Querfurt/Sachsen geboren. Studium der Malerei in München, Kontakt zur Künstlergruppe „Blauer Reiter" und in Berlin zur Galerie „Der Sturm". 1916 Lehrer an der Kunstschule des „Sturm" in Berlin. 1919 Berufung ans Staatliche Bauhaus Weimar, pädagogischer Aufbau und Organisationsfragen. 1923 Lehrer des Vorkurses im Wechsel mit Johannes Itten. 1923–25 Leiter der Webereiwerkstatt. 1923 Organisation der ersten Bauhausausstellung in Weimar, Entwurf des Ausstellungsgebäudes „Haus Am Horn". 1924 Studienreise in die USA. 1925–27 Künstlerischer Leiter der Webereiwerkstatt am Bauhaus Dessau. 1926 Experimental-Stahlhaus nahe der Siedlung Dessau-Törten gemeinsam mit Richard Paulick. 1927–31 Lehrer an der Ittenschule in Berlin. 1931–33 Professor für Malerei an der Breslauer Akademie für Kunst und Kunstgewerbe. 1933 zunächst entlassen, dann wieder eingestellt. 1939–58 Leitung der Meisterklasse für Textilkunst an der Krefelder Textilingenieurschule, Arbeit als freier Maler. 1987 in Lindau/Bodensee gestorben.

Georg Muche (1895–1987) Painter, Born 1895 in Querfurt, Saxony. Studied painting in Munich. Contact with the "Der Blaue Reiter" art group and the "Der Sturm" gallery in Berlin. 1916 Tutor at the "Der Sturm" art school in Berlin. 1919 Appointment at the Staatliche Bauhaus Weimar, development of educational and organisational facets. 1923 Preliminary course tutor, sharing a position with Johannes Itten. 1923–25 Head of the textile workshop. 1923 Organisation of the first Bauhaus exhibition in Weimar, design of the exhibition building "Haus Am Horn". 1924 Study trip to the USA. 1925–27 Artistic head of the textile workshop at the Bauhaus in Dessau. 1926 Collaboration with Richard Paulick on an experimental steel house near the Dessau-Törten Estate. 1927–31 Tutor at the Ittenschule in Berlin. 1931–33 Professor of painting at the Akademie für Kunst und Kunstgewerbe in Breslau. 1933 Dismissed, then reinstated. 1939–58 Head of the textile art Master class art at the Textilingenieurschule in Krefeld, freelance painter. Died 1987 in Lindau, Bodensee.

Richard Paulick (1903–1979) Architekt, Stadtplaner, 1903 in Roßlau/Elbe geboren. 1923–27 Studium der Architektur in Dresden und Berlin. Kontakte zum Staatlichen Bauhaus Weimar, Freundschaft mit Georg Muche. Entwürfe von Stahltypenhäusern, 1926 Experimental-Stahlhaus in Dessau, Mitarbeit am Bau der Siedlung Dessau-Törten. 1927–30 Baubüro von Walter Gropius in Dessau, ab 1928 dessen Leiter. Übernahme der Bauleitung des Arbeitsamtes. 1930 eigenes Büro in Dessau, Bau von sieben Mietshausblocks im Süden Dessaus im Auftrag der Deutschen Wohnungsfürsorgegesellschaft. 1933 Emigration nach China, einflussreicher Architekt, Hochschullehrer und Stadtplaner in Shanghai. 1950 Übersiedlung in die DDR. Wiederaufbau der Staatsoper Unter den Linden in Berlin, Beteiligung am Bau der Berliner Stalinallee und beim Wiederaufbau Dresdens. Chefarchitekt u. a. von Hoyerswerda und Halle-Neustadt. 1979 in Berlin gestorben.

Richard Paulick (1903–1979) Architect, town planner, Born 1903 in Rosslau/Elbe. 1923–27 Studied architecture in Dresden and Berlin. Contacts with the Staatliches Bauhaus Weimar, friendship with Georg Muche. Design of prototype steel houses. 1926 Experimental steel house in Dessau, collaboration on the construction of the Dessau-Törten Estate. 1927–30 Walter Gropius' office in Dessau, its head from 1928, construction manager of the Employment Office. 1930 Own office in Dessau, construction of seven tenement blocks in south Dessau on behalf of the Deutsche Wohnungsfürsorgegesellschaft. 1933 Emigration to China, influential architect, tutor and town planner in Shanghai. 1950 Relocation to the GDR. Post-war reconstruction of the State Opera Unter den Linden in Berlin, participation in the construction of the Stalinallee in Berlin and post-war reconstruction in Dresden. Head architect of, among others, Hoyerswerda and Halle-Neustadt. Died 1979 in Berlin.

Walter Peterhans (1897–1960) Fotograf, 1897 in Frankfurt/Main geboren. 1914–20 Kriegsdienst und Gefangenschaft. 1920–23 Studium von Maschinenbau, Philosophie, Mathematik und Kunstgeschichte. 1925–26 Studium der Fotografischen Reproduktions- und Druckverfahren in Leipzig, Fotografenmeisterprüfung. Ab 1926 freischaffend als Industrie- und Porträtfotograf in Berlin, Schülerinnen u. a. Grete Stern und Ellen Auerbach. 1929 Berufung ans Bauhaus Dessau, Aufbau und Leitung der Fotoklasse, 1932–33 im Bauhaus Berlin. 1933–38 Lehrer an Werner Graeffs Fotoschule, später an der Reimann-Schule in Berlin. 1938 Emigration in die USA, bis 1960 Professor für Visuelles Training, Analyse und Kunstgeschichte an der Architekturabteilung des Armour Institute in Chicago, später am Illinois Institute of Technology. 1945–47 Research Associate für Philosophie an der Universität in Chicago. 1953 Gastprofessor an der Hochschule für Gestaltung in Ulm. 1960 in der Nähe von Stuttgart gestorben.

Walter Peterhans (1897–1960) Photographer, Born 1897 in Frankfurt/Main. 1914–20 Military service and imprisonment. 1920–23 Studied mechanical engineering, mathematics and art history. 1925–26 Studied photographic reproduction and printing processes in Leipzig, Master's certificate in photography. From 1926 Self-employed as an industrial and portrait photographer in Berlin, students included Grete Stern and Ellen Auerbach. 1929 Appointment at the Bauhaus in Dessau, building up and leading the photography course. 1932–33 At the Bauhaus in Berlin. 1933–38 Tutor at the Werner Graeff photography school, later the Reimann-Schule, in Berlin. 1938 Emigration to the USA. To 1960 Professor of Visual Training, Analysis and Art History at the Department of Architecture of the Armour Institute in Chicago, later at the Illinois Institute of Technology. 1945–47 Research Associate for philosophy at the University in Chicago. 1953 Guest professor at the Hochschule für Gestaltung in Ulm. Died 1960 near Stuttgart.

Lilly Reich (1885–1947) Architektin, Designerin, 1885 in Berlin geboren. Ausbildung als Kurbelstickerin, dann Studium u. a. in den Wiener Werkstätten. 1912 Mitglied im Deutschen Werkbund, 1920 erste Frau in dessen Vorstand. Gestaltung von Ausstellungen für den Werkbund. Bis 1924 Atelier für Innenraumgestaltung, Dekorationskunst und Mode in Berlin. Bis 1926 Atelier für Ausstellungsgestaltung und Mode in Frankfurt/Main. 1927 Teilnahme an der Werkbundausstellung „Die Wohnung" in Stuttgart-Weißenhof, Gestaltung von Ausstellungshallen und Innenräumen, auch in Zusammenarbeit mit Ludwig Mies van der Rohe. 1932–33 Leiterin der Weberei und der Ausbauabteilung des Bauhauses in Dessau und Berlin. Bis 1937 Aufträge zur Ausstellungsgestaltung, 1939 dienstverpflichtet bei der Organisation Todt. 1945–46 Dozentin für Raumgestaltung und Gebäudelehre an der Hochschule für Bildende Künste in Berlin. Atelier für Architektur, Design, Textilien und Mode. 1947 in Berlin gestorben.

Lilly Reich (1885–1947) Architect, designer, Born 1885 in Berlin. Trained as a specialist embroiderer, later studied in, among others, the Wiener Werkstätten. 1912 Member of the Deutsche Werkbund, 1920 first female member of its executive committee. Exhibition designer for the Werkbund. To 1924 Studio for interior design, decoration and fashion in Berlin. To 1926 Studio for exhibition design and fashion in Frankfurt/Main. 1927 Participation in the Werkbund exhibition "Die Wohnung" in Stuttgart-Weißenhof, design of exhibition spaces and interiors, some in collaboration with Ludwig Mies van der Rohe. 1932–33 Head of the Bauhaus textile workshops and construction departments in Dessau and Berlin. To 1937 Commissions for exhibition design. 1939 Compulsory work for the Organisation Todt. 1945–46 Lecturer in spatial design and architectural theory at the Hochschule für Bildende Künste in Berlin. Studio for architecture, design, textiles and fashion. Died 1947 in Berlin.

Grete Reichardt (1907–1984) Weberin, Textildesignerin, 1907 in Erfurt geboren, dort 1921–25 Besuch der Handwerker- und Kunstgewerbeschule. 1926 Immatrikulation am Bauhaus Dessau, Vorkurs bei Josef Albers und László Moholy-Nagy, Unterricht bei Paul Klee, Wassily Kandinsky und Joost Schmidt. 1926–1931 Weberei bei Gunta Stölzl, 1929 Gesellenprüfung vor der Handwerkskammer Dessau, Außensemester in Königsberg. Ab 1930 freie Mitarbeiterin der Weberei, 1931 Bauhaus-Diplom. Mitwirkung an der Ausstattung der Bundesschule des Allgemeinen Deutschen Gewerkschaftsbundes (ADGB) in Bernau bei Berlin und beim Operncafé in Dessau. Maßgeblicher Anteil an der Entwicklung des Eisengarngewebes. 1931–32 Arbeit als Grafikerin und Weberin in den Niederlanden. 1933 Rückkehr nach Erfurt, 1934 Gründung der Handweberei Grete Reichardt, 1942 Meisterprüfung. Zahlreiche Auszeichnungen seit den 1930er Jahren. 1969 Ehrenurkunde des Ministeriums für Kultur der DDR. 1984 in Erfurt gestorben.

Grete Reichardt (1907–1984) Weaver, textile designer, Born 1907 in Erfurt. From 1921–25 Attended the Handwerker- und Kunstgewerbeschule.

1926 Enrolment at the Bauhaus in Dessau, preliminary course under Josef Albers and László Moholy-Nagy, tuition with Paul Klee, Wassily Kandinsky and Joost Schmidt. 1926–1931 Textile workshop under Gunta Stölzl, 1929 Journeyman's certificate from the chamber of trade in Dessau, external semester in Königsberg. From 1930 Freelance work in the weaving workshop. 1931 Bauhaus diploma. Collaboration on the interior design of the Bundesschule des Allgemeinen Deutschen Gewerkschaftsbundes (ADGB) in Bernau near Berlin and the Opera Café in Dessau. Significant participant in the development of the Eisengarngewebe (iron yarn) textile. 1931–32 Work as a graphic designer and weaver in the Netherlands. 1933 Return to Erfurt. 1934 Foundation of the company Handweberei Grete Reichardt. 1942 Master's certificate. Numerous awards from the 1930s. 1969 Honorary award by the Ministry for Culture of the GDR. Died 1984 in Erfurt.

Xanti Schawinski (1904–1979) Maler, Typograf, Bühnenbildner, 1904 in Basel/Schweiz geboren. 1921–23 Architekturausbildung in Köln, 1922–23 Kunstgewerbeschule in Berlin. 1924 Immatrikulation am Staatlichen Bauhaus Weimar, Vorkurs bei László Moholy-Nagy. 1925–28 am Bauhaus Dessau Kurse bei Wassily Kandinsky und Paul Klee, Assistent von Oskar Schlemmer in der Bühnenwerkstatt. 1925 Mitglied der Bauhaus-Kapelle, spielte Banjo, Flexaton, Lotusflöte und Saxophon. 1929–31 Grafiker bei der Stadt Magdeburg, 1933–36 freier Werbegrafiker in Italien. 1936 Emigration in die USA, bis 1938 Lehrer am Black Mountain College in Ashville, North Carolina, Leitung u. a. einer Bühnenklasse. Ab 1938 Ausstellungs- und Werbegestalter in New York. 1943–46 Dozent für Grafikdesign und Malerei am New York City College. Ab 1946 freier Künstler. 1950–54 Lehrauftrag in verschiedenen künstlerischen Fächern an der New York University. Ab 1961 zahlreiche Ausstellungen in Europa. 1979 in Locarno/Schweiz gestorben.

Xanti Schawinski (1904–1979) Painter, typographer, stage designer, Born 1904 in Basel, Switzerland. 1921–23 Studied architecture in Cologne, 1922–23 at the Kunstgewerbeschule in Berlin. 1924 Enrolment at the Staatliches Bauhaus Weimar, preliminary course under László Moholy-Nagy. 1925–28 At the Bauhaus in Dessau, tuition with Wassily Kandinsky and Paul Klee, assistant to Oskar Schlemmer in the theatre workshop. 1925 Member of the Bauhaus band, played banjo, flexatone, lotus flute and saxophone. 1929–31 Graphic designer for the city of Magdeburg. 1933–36 Freelance commercial artist in Italy. 1936 Emigration to the USA, tutor at Black Mountain College in Ashville, North Carolina, head of a stage course among others to 1938. From 1938 Exhibition and advertising design in New York. 1943–46 Lecturer in graphic design and painting at New York City College. From 1946 Freelance artist. 1950–54 Lectureships in various artistic disciplines at New York University. From 1961 Numerous exhibitions in Europe. Died 1979 in Locarno, Switzerland.

Hinnerk Scheper (1897–1957) Maler, Farbgestalter, Denkmalpfleger, 1897 in Badbergen/Osnabrück geboren. 1918–19 Kunstgewerbeschule und Kunstakademie Düsseldorf und Kunstgewerbeschule Bremen. 1919 Immatrikulation am Staatlichen Bauhaus Weimar, Vorkurs bei Johannes Itten. 1920–22 Wandmalereiwerkstatt bei Johannes Itten und Oskar Schlemmer, Unterricht bei Paul Klee. 1922 Malermeisterprüfung, bis 1925 selbstständiger Maler. 1925 Berufung ans Bauhaus Dessau, bis 1933 Leiter der Wandmalereiwerkstatt, ab 1931 des Farbunterrichtes. Farbgestaltungen u. a. für das Bauhaus und das Museum Folkwang in Essen. 1929 und 1931 in Moskau, u. a. Farbgestaltung für Haus Narkomfin, Aufbau eines Bauinstitutes, Fertigung von Fotoserien und Reportagen. Nach 1933 freier Maler und Restaurator in Berlin, Kriegsdienst. 1945 Leiter des Amtes für Denkmalpflege in Berlin, ab 1953 Landeskonservator. 1957 in Berlin gestorben.

Hinnerk Scheper (1897–1957) Painter, colour designer, conservationist, Born 1897 in Badbergen/Osnabrück. 1918–19 Attended the Kunstgewerbeschule and Kunstakademie in Düsseldorf and the Kunstgewerbeschule in Bremen. 1919 Enrolment at the Staatliche Bauhaus Weimar, preliminary course under Johannes Itten. 1920–22 Wall painting workshop with Johannes Itten and Oskar Schlemmer, tuition with Paul Klee. 1922 Master's certificate in painting, to 1925 self-employed painter. 1925 Appointment at the Bauhaus in Dessau, to 1933 head of the wall painting workshop and, from 1931, of colour theory. Colour design for, among others, the Bauhaus and the Folkwang Museum in Essen. 1929 and 1931 in Moscow, colour design for, among others, the Narkomfin House, foundation of an architectural institute, production of a number of photo series and reports. From 1933 Freelance painter and restorer in Berlin, military service. 1945 Head of the Berlin office for the preservation of monuments. From 1953 State conservation officer. Died 1957 in Berlin

Oskar Schlemmer (1888–1943) Maler, Bildhauer, Bühnenbildner, 1888 in Stuttgart geboren. Malereistudium an der dortigen Akademie, 1912 Meisterschüler von Adolf Hölzel. 1921 Berufung ans Staatliche Bauhaus Weimar. 1922 Uraufführung des Triadischen Balletts in Stuttgart. 1921–23 abwechselnd mit Johannes Itten Leiter der Wandmalereiwerkstatt. Leitung der Steinbildhauerei, später auch der Holzbildhauerei, Unterricht im Aktzeichnen. 1923–29 Leiter der Bühnenwerkstatt in Weimar und Dessau. 1927 Unterricht im Figurenzeichnen, ab 1928 Unterricht „Der Mensch". 1928–29 Tournee mit der Bauhausbühne durch Deutschland. 1929 Berufung an die Breslauer Akademie für Kunst und Kunstgewerbe, 1932 an die Vereinigten Staatsschulen für Kunst und Kunstgewerbe nach Berlin. 1933 Entlassung durch die Nationalsozialisten, kurze Übersiedlung in die Schweiz. 1938 Arbeit in einem Stuttgarter Malergeschäft, 1939–40 Aufträge für Tarnanstriche von Kasernen etc. 1940 Einrichtung eines Versuchslabors in einer Wuppertaler Lackfabrik. 1943 in Baden-Baden gestorben.

Oskar Schlemmer (1888–1943) Painter, sculptor, stage designer, Born 1888 in Stuttgart. Studied painting at the Stuttgart academy. 1912 Masters' course under Adolf Hölzel. 1921 Appointment at the Staatliches Bauhaus Weimar. 1922 Premiere of the triadic ballet in Stuttgart. 1921–23 Joint head of the wall painting workshop with Johannes Itten. Head of the stone carving department, later also the wood carving department, tuition in life drawing. 1923–29 Head of the theatre workshop in Weimar and Dessau. 1927 Tuition in figure drawing. From 1928 Tutors the class "Der Mensch" (The Human Being). 1928–29 Tour of Germany with the Bauhaus theatre. 1929 Appointment at the Akademie für Kunst und Kunstgewerbe in Breslau, 1932 at the Vereinigte Staatsschulen für Kunst und Kunstgewerbe in Berlin. 1933 Dismissal by the National Socialists, brief relocation to Switzerland. 1938 Work in a painting firm in Stuttgart. 1939–40 Commissions for camouflaging barracks etc. 1940 Foundation of an experimental laboratory in a paint factory in Wuppertal. Died 1943 in Baden-Baden.

Joost Schmidt (1893–1948) Grafiker, Maler, 1893 in Wunstorf geboren. 1910–14 Kunststudium in Weimar. 1914–18 Kriegsdienst und Gefangenschaft. 1919 Immatrikulation am Staatlichen Bauhaus Weimar. 1919–25 Lehre in der Holz- und Steinbildhauerei bei Johannes Itten und Oskar Schlemmer. 1925 Gesellenprüfung vor der Handwerkskammer Weimar und Berufung zum Jungmeister. 1925 am Bauhaus Dessau Übernahme der Plastischen Werkstatt, Unterricht in Schriftgestaltung. 1928–32 Leiter der Abteilung für Reklame, Typografie und Druckerei, ab 1929 mit angeschlossener Fotoabteilung. Gestaltung u. a. von Broschüren, Geschäftspapieren, Katalogen. 1929–30 Lehrer für Aktzeichnen. Nach 1933 Ausstellungsgestaltungen gemeinsam mit Walter Gropius. 1935 Verbot seiner Lehrtätigkeit an der Reimann-Schule in Berlin. 1945 Berufung als Professor für Architektur an die Hochschule für Bildende Künste in Berlin, Lehrer des Vorkurses für Architektur. 1948 in Nürnberg gestorben.

Joost Schmidt (1893–1948) Graphic designer, painter, Born 1893 in Wunstorf. 1910–14 Studied art in Weimar. 1914–18 Military service and imprisonment. 1919 Enrolment at the Staatliches Bauhaus Weimar. 1919–25 Apprenticeship in stone and wood carving workshop under Johannes Itten and Oskar Schlemmer. 1925 Master's certificate from the chamber of trade in Weimar and appointment as a Junior Master. 1925 At the Bauhaus in Dessau, head of the sculpture workshop, typography tutor. 1928–32 Head of the advertising, typography and printing department, and from 1929, of the incorporated photography department. Design of, i.e., brochures, business papers and catalogues. 1929–30 Life drawing tutor. From 1933 Exhibition design in collaboration with Walter Gropius. 1935 Teaching ban at Reimann-Schule in Berlin. 1945 Appointment as professor of architecture at the Hochschule für Bildende Künste in Berlin, tutor of the preliminary course in architecture. Died 1948 in Nuremberg.

Gunta Stadler-Stölzl, geb. Stölzl (1897–1983) Weberin, Textildesignerin, 1897 in München geboren, Studium an der dortigen Kunstgewerbeschule. 1916–18 Rotkreuzschwester. 1919 Immatrikulation am Staatlichen Bauhaus Weimar; Vorkurs, Glasmalerei- und Wandmalereiwerkstatt bei Johannes Itten. 1920–21 Frauenklasse bei Johannes Itten und Helene Börner. 1921–25 Webereiwerkstatt bei Georg Muche, Unterricht bei Paul Klee. 1923 Gesellenprüfung als Weberin vor der Handwerkskammer Weimar, Aufbau der Färberei. 1925 am Bauhaus Dessau Werkmeisterin der Weberei, 1927–31 Übernahme der Werkstatt als Jungmeisterin. 1928 Reise mit anderen Bauhäuslern nach Moskau. 1931 Weggang vom Bauhaus, Übersiedlung in die Schweiz. 1932–67 Arbeit in der eigenen Handweberei, zeitweise gemeinsam mit anderen Bauhäuslern. 1937 Auszeichnung auf der Pariser Weltausstellung. 1983 in Küsnacht/Schweiz gestorben.

Gunta Stadler-Stölzl, born Stölzl (1897–1983) Weaver, textile designer, Born 1897 in Munich, studied at the Kunstgewerbeschule in Munich. 1916–18 Red Cross nurse. 1919 Enrolment at the Staatliches Bauhaus Weimar; preliminary course, glass painting and wall painting workshop under Johannes Itten. 1920–21 Frauenklasse (female-only course) with Johannes Itten and Helene Börner. 1921–25 Textile workshop under Georg Muche, tuition with Paul Klee. 1923 Journeyman's certificate as a weaver from the chamber of trade in Weimar, foundation of the dye works. 1925 At the Bauhaus Dessau, Technical Master of the textile workshop, 1927–31 becomes head of the workshop as a Junior Master. 1928 Trip with other Bauhaus associates to Moscow. 1931 Departure from the Bauhaus, relocation to Switzerland. 1932–67 Work in her handmade textile business, at times with other Bauhaus associates. 1937 Award at the Paris World Fair. Died 1983 in Küsnacht, Switzerland.

Wilhelm Wagenfeld (1900–1990) Industriedesigner, 1900 in Bremen geboren. 1916–19 Kunstgewerbeschule in Bremen, 1919–22 Ausbildung zum Silberschmied. 1923 Immatrikulation am Staatlichen Bauhaus Weimar, Vorkurs bei Josef Albers und László Moholy-Nagy. 1923–25 Lehre in der Metallwerkstatt bei László Moholy-Nagy, Unterricht bei Wassily Kandinsky und Paul Klee. 1924 Gesellenprüfung als Silberschmied und Ziseleur. Gemeinsam mit Carl Jakob Jucker Entwurf für die Tischleuchte aus Metall und Glas, heute als „Bauhaus-Leuchte" bekannt. 1925–28 Assistent an der Staatlichen Hochschule für Handwerk und Baukunst in Weimar, Nachfolgeeinrichtung des Staatlichen Bauhauses. 1928–30 dort Leiter der Metallwerkstatt, 1930 gekündigt auf Drängen der NSDAP in Thüringen. 1931–35 Dozent an der Staatlichen Kunsthochschule Berlin-Schöneberg. Freiberuflich tätig, u. a. im Jenaer Glaswerk Schott & Gen. 1935–47 künstlerischer Leiter der Vereinigten Lausitzer Glaswerke, Auszeichnungen in Paris und Mailand. Nach 1945 Lehrer an der Berliner Hochschule für Bildende Künste, Referent für industrielle Formgebung in Stuttgart. 1950–77 Zusammenarbeit mit der Württembergischen Metallwarenfabrik AG (WMF). 1954–78 Versuchs- und Entwicklungsanstalt für Industriemodelle, Entwürfe für Firmen wie Braun, die Pelikan-Werke oder die Rosenthal-Porzellan AG. 1990 in Stuttgart gestorben.

Wilhelm Wagenfeld (1900–1990) Industrial designer, Born 1900 in Bremen. 1916–19 Kunstgewerbeschule in Bremen. 1919–22 Silversmith's apprenticeship. 1923 Enrolment at the Staatliches Bauhaus Weimar, preliminary course under Josef Albers and László Moholy-Nagy. 1923–25 Apprenticeship in the metal workshop under László Moholy-Nagy, tuition with Wassily Kandinsky and Paul Klee. 1924 Master's certificate as a silversmith and engraver. Collaboration with Carl Jakob Jucker, design of the metal and glass table lamp known today as the "Bauhaus lamp". 1925–28 Assistant at the Staatliche Hochschule für Handwerk und Baukunst in Weimar, the successor of the Staatliches Bauhaus. 1928–30 Head of the metal workshop there, dismissed in 1930 at the insistence of the NSDAP in Thuringia. 1931–35 Lecturer at the Staatliche Kunsthochschule in Berlin-Schöneberg. Freelance, working in, among others, the glass factory Jenaer Glaswerk Schott & Gen in Jena. 1935–47 Artistic head of the Vereinigte Lausitzer Glaswerke glass factory, awards in Paris and Milan. From 1945 Tutor at the Berlin Hochschule für Bildende Künste, consultant for industrial shaping technology in Stuttgart. 1950–77 Collaboration with the metals factory Württembergische Metallwarenfabrik AG (WMF). 1954–78 Research and development institute for industrial models, design for firms such as Braun, Pelikan-Werke and Rosenthal-Porzellan AG. Died 1990 in Stuttgart.

Picture Credits **Bildnachweis**

Cover
Tür, Wand und Steinholzestrich im
Nordflügel
Door, wall and magnesite floor in the
north wing
Foto: Doreen Ritzau / Stiftung Bau-
haus Dessau, 2006

Umschlaginnenseiten Endpaper
Vorn front
Grundrisse des Bauhausgebäudes,
Sockelgeschoss, Erdgeschoss
Floor plan of the Bauhaus Building,
basement, ground floor
Stiftung Bauhaus Dessau, 1999/2006
Hinten back
Grundrisse des Bauhausgebäudes, 1.
Obergeschoss, 2. Obergeschoss
Floor plan of the Bauhaus Building,
first floor, second floor
Stiftung Bauhaus Dessau, 1999/2006

Einführung Introduction
Seite/Page 18:
Ateliergebäude bei Nacht
Studio building by night
Foto: Martin Brück / Stiftung Bauhaus
Dessau, 2005

Seite/Page 20:
Werkstattflügel von Süden
Workshop wing from the south
Foto: F.-H. Müller / Stiftung Bauhaus
Dessau, 2006

Seite/Page 22:
Glasvorhangfassade mit Südeingang
Glass curtain wall and south entrance
Foto: Kirsten Baumann / Stiftung
Bauhaus Dessau, 2006

Seite/Page 23:
Transparente Ecke des Werkstattflü-
gels
Transparent corner of the workshop
wing
Foto: Kirsten Baumann / Stiftung
Bauhaus Dessau, 2005

Seiten/Pages 24/25:
Bauhausgebäude von Westen
Bauhaus Building from the west
Foto: F.-H. Müller / Stiftung Bauhaus
Dessau, 2006

Seite/Page 26:
Eingang Bauhaus Dessau
Entrance Bauhaus Dessau
Foto: Kirsten Baumann / Stiftung
Bauhaus Dessau, 2006

Seite/Page 27; Umschlagrückseite/
Back cover (r.):
Eingang Bauhaus Dessau
Entrance Bauhaus Dessau
Foto: Kirsten Baumann / Stiftung
Bauhaus Dessau, 2006

Seite/Page 28:
Detail Glasvorhangfassade
Detail, curtain wall
Foto: Doreen Ritzau / Stiftung Bau-
haus Dessau, 2006

Seite/Page 29:
Detail des Schriftzuges an der
Südseite
Detail, lettering on the south side of
the building
Foto: Doreen Ritzau / Stiftung Bau-
haus Dessau, 2006

Seite/Page 30:
Balkone an der Ostseite des Atelier-
gebäudes
Balconies on the east side of the
studio building
Foto: Kirsten Baumann / Stiftung
Bauhaus Dessau, 2005

Seite/Page 31:
Balkone an der Südseite des Atelier-
gebäudes
Balconies on the south side of the
studio building
Foto: Doreen Ritzau / Stiftung Bauhaus Dessau, 2006

Seite/Page 32:
Südseite des Werkstattflügels
South side of the workshop wing
Foto: Doreen Ritzau / Stiftung Bau-
haus Dessau, 2006

Seite/Page 33:
Treppenaufgang zur Mensaterrasse
Staircase leading to the canteen
terrace
Foto: Doreen Ritzau / Stiftung Bau-
haus Dessau, 2006

Festebene Festive area
Seite/Page 34:
Vestibül mit Treppenaufgang
Entrance area and staircase
Foto: Doreen Ritzau / Stiftung Bau-
haus Dessau, 2006

Seite/Page 36 oben/top:
Vestibül im Erdgeschoss
Entrance area on the ground floor
Foto: Doreen Ritzau / Stiftung Bau-
haus Dessau, 2006

Seite/Page 36 unten/bottom:
Soffittenleuchten (Entwurf: Max Krajewski) und Farbgebung der Decke
im Vestibül
Tubular lights (design: Max Krajewski) and ceiling colour design in the
entrance area
Foto: Doreen Ritzau / Stiftung Bauhaus Dessau, 2006

Seite/Page 38:
Fußbodendetail im Vestibül
Floor detail in the entrance area
Foto: Doreen Ritzau / Stiftung Bau-
haus Dessau, 2006

Seite/Page 39:
Vestibül, Junkers-Heizkörper, Eingang
zum Werkstattflügel
Entrance area, Junkers radiator,
entrance to the workshop wing
Foto: Doreen Ritzau / Stiftung Bauhaus Dessau, 2006

Seite/Page 40 oben/top:
Fensteröffnungsmechanismus in der
Festebene, Detail
Window opening mechanism in the
festive area, detail
Foto: Doreen Ritzau / Stiftung Bau-
haus Dessau, 2006

Seite/Page 40 unten/bottom:
Metallbeschlag und Holzgriff der
Aulatür
Metal detail and wooden handle,
auditorium door
Foto: Doreen Ritzau / Stiftung Bau-
haus Dessau, 2006

Ausbildung Education

Seite/Page 98:
Lehrplan des Bauhaus Dessau, Vor- und Rückansicht, 1925
Bauhaus Dessau curriculum, front and back view, 1925
Unbekannt (Entwurf), Druck- und Reklamewerkstatt des Bauhauses Weimar oder Dessau (Herstellung) / Stiftung Bauhaus Dessau / Foto: Kelly Kellerhoff

Seite/Page 99:
Konrad Püschel, Grätenfaltung, Materialübung aus dem Vorkurs bei Josef Albers, 1926/27
Konrad Püschel, zigzag folding technique, exercise from Josef Albers' preliminary course, 1926/27
Konrad Püschel (Entwurf) / Stiftung Bauhaus Dessau / Foto: Kelly Kellerhoff

Seite/Page 100:
Rudolf Ortner, Das wachsende Haus, Wettbewerbsentwurf (Blatt 3), 1931/32
Rudolf Ortner, "The Growing House", competition draft (Page 3), 1931/32
Rudolf Ortner (Entwurf) / Stiftung Bauhaus Dessau / Foto: Sebastian Kaps / © Annalies Ortner-Bach

Seite/Page 101:
Hugo Clausing, Meisterhäuser Dessau, Direktorenhaus, Ansichten mit eingezeichnetem Schattenwurf der Morgensonne. Übung aus dem Unterricht in darstellender Geometrie bei Friedrich Köhn, 1928
Hugo Clausing, Dessau Masters' Houses, Directors' House, perspectives showing shadows created by the morning sun. Exercise from a class in illustrative geometry by Friedrich Köhn, 1928
Hugo Clausing (Entwurf) / Stiftung Bauhaus Dessau / Foto: Kelly Kellerhoff / © Brigitte Seiferth

Seite/Page 102:
Gestentanz III, Szenenaufnahmen mit Oskar Schlemmer, Werner Siedhoff und Walter Kaminsky, 1927
Gesture dance III, photo of a scene with Oskar Schlemmer, Werner Siedhoff and Walter Kaminsky, 1927
Foto: Erich Consemüller / Bühnen Archiv Oskar Schlemmer / Bauhaus-Archiv Berlin / © Janine Schlemmer, München (Deutschland) / © Ute Jaina Schlemmer, Oggebbio (Italien) / © Dr. Stephan Consemüller

Seite/Page 103:
László Moholy-Nagy, Prospekt für die Bauhausbücher, 1928
László Moholy-Nagy, brochure for the Bauhaus books, 1928
László Moholy-Nagy / Stiftung Bauhaus Dessau / Foto: Kelly Kellerhoff / © VG BILD-KUNST, Bonn 2007

Seite/Page 104:
Edmund Collein, Das Innere eines Konzertflügels, 1928
Edmund Collein, "The interior of a grand piano", 1928
Foto: Edmund Collein / Stiftung Bauhaus Dessau / Foto (Reproduktion): Kelly Kellerhoff / © Ursula Kirsten-Collein

Seite/Page 105:
Eugen Batz, Gewinkelt. Aus der Malklasse bei Paul Klee, 1930
Eugen Batz, "Gewinkelt", from a painting class given by Paul Klee, 1930
Eugen Batz / Stiftung Bauhaus Dessau / Foto: Kelly Kellerhoff / © Galerie Döbele, Dresden

Seite/Page 106 links/left:
Marianne Brandt, Sahnegießer, Zuckerschale und Tablett, Silber, 1928
Marianne Brandt, cream jug, sugar bowl and tray, silver, 1928
Marianne Brandt (Entwurf) / Stiftung Bauhaus Dessau / Foto: Kelly Kellerhoff / © VG BILD-KUNST, Bonn 2007

Seite/Page 106 rechts/right:
Marianne Brandt, Hin Bredendieck, Kandem-Schreibtischleuchte
Marianne Brandt, Hin Bredendieck, "Kandem" desk lamp
Marianne Brandt, Hin Bredendieck (Entwurf, 1928), Körting & Mathiesen AG (Herstellung, 1929) / Stiftung Bauhaus Dessau / Foto: Kelly Kellerhoff / © VG BILD-KUNST, Bonn 2007 / Karl Bredendieck, Cork (Irland)

Seite/Page 107:
Grete Reichardt, Teppich für ein Kinderzimmer, 1929 entworfen, 1977 hergestellt
Grete Reichardt, carpet for a child's room, designed 1929, manufactured 1977
Grete Reichardt (Entwurf und Herstellung) / Stiftung Bauhaus Dessau / Foto: Kelly Kellerhoff / © Gisela Kaiser

Seite/Page 108:
Marcel Breuer, Clubsessel, Prototyp des späteren B3, 1925/26
Marcel Breuer, Club Chair, early prototype of the B3, 1925/26
Marcel Breuer / Stiftung Bauhaus Dessau / Foto: Kelly Kellerhoff / © Kontakt: Thomas Breuer, New York

Seite/Page 109:
Carl Fieger, Schlafzimmereinrichtung für Haus Fieger, 1927
Carl Fieger, bedroom furniture for the Fieger house, 1927
Carl Fieger (Entwurf), Tischlereiwerkstatt des Bauhauses (Herstellung) / Stiftung Bauhaus Dessau / Foto: Kelly Kellerhoff

Seite/Page 110:
Franz Ehrlich, Architekturentwurf mit farbiger Wandgestaltung, um 1930
Franz Ehrlich, Architectural draft with coloured wall design, ca. 1930
Franz Ehrlich (Entwurf) / Stiftung Bauhaus Dessau / Foto: Peter Kühn / © Volkmar Haak

Seite/Page 111:
Grete Reichardt, Tapetenentwurf, um 1930
Grete Reichardt, wallpaper design, ca. 1930
Grete Reichardt (Entwurf) / Stiftung Bauhaus Dessau / Foto: Kelly Kellerhoff / © Gisela Kaiser

Bauhaus und Bauhäusler nach 1932/33 Bauhaus and Bauhaus people after 1932/33
Seite/Page 114:
Otti Berger in der Mensa des Bauhausgebäudes am 30. September 1932, einen Tag vor der Schließung der Schule
Otti Berger in the Bauhaus canteen on September 30th, 1932, one day before the school's closure
Foto: Gertrud Arndt / Stiftung Bauhaus Dessau / © Archiv Alfred und Gertrud Arndt, Darmstadt / Foto (Reproduktion): Kelly Kellerhoff

Seite/Page 116:
Festgestaltung der Mensa durch die Landesfrauenarbeitsschule, um 1935
Festive decoration of the canteen by women from the Landesfrauenarbeitsschule, ca. 1935
Foto: Unbekannt / Stiftung Bauhaus Dessau

Kurzporträts Biographies
Seite/Page 120:
Anni Albers, ca. 1929
Foto: Otto Umbehr (Umbo) / Bauhaus-Archiv Berlin / © Galerie Kicken, Berlin

Josef Albers, frühe 1930er Jahre
Foto: Unbekannt / Bauhaus-Archiv Berlin

Alfred Arndt, 1929
Foto: Gertrud Arndt / Bauhaus-Archiv Berlin / © Archiv Alfred und Gertrud Arndt, Darmstadt

Gertrud Arndt, Selbstporträt (Ausschnitt), 1926
Foto: Bauhaus-Archiv Berlin / © Archiv Alfred und Gertrud Arndt, Darmstadt

Herbert Bayer, 1927
Foto: Irene Bayer / Bauhaus-Archiv Berlin

Max Bill, 1960er Jahre
Foto: Frank Larese, St. Gallen (Schweiz)

Marianne Brandt, um 1933
Foto: Fritz Lafeldt / Stiftung Bauhaus Dessau

Marcel Breuer, um 1928
Foto: Unbekannt / Stiftung Bauhaus Dessau

Edmund Collein, um 1928
Foto: Unbekannt

Erich Consemüller, um 1924
Foto: Unbekannt

Franz Ehrlich, um 1932
Foto: Unbekannt

Lyonel Feininger, 1928
Foto: Unbekannt / Bauhaus-Archiv Berlin

Carl Fieger, ca. 1935
Foto: Unbekannt (Ausschnitt) / Stiftung Bauhaus Dessau

Walter Gropius, ca. 1922
Foto: Louis Held, Weimar

Ludwig Grote, ca. 1930
Foto: Unbekannt

Fritz Hesse, 1932
Foto: Unbekannt

Ludwig Hilberseimer, frühe 1930er Jahre
Foto: Dephot / Bauhaus-Archiv Berlin

Seite/Page 121:
Johannes Itten, um 1921
Foto: Paula Stockmar (Ausschnitt)

Hugo Junkers, ca. 1930
Foto: Unbekannt / Stadtarchiv Dessau

Wassily Kandinsky, frühe 1930er Jahre
Foto: Hugo Erfurth / © VG BILD-KUNST, Bonn 2007

Paul Klee, 1927
Foto: Hugo Erfurth / Bauhaus-Archiv Berlin / © VG BILD-KUNST, Bonn 2007

Max Krajewski, ca. 1927
Foto: Unbekannt

Hannes Meyer, um 1928
Foto: Otto Umbehr (Umbo) / Bauhaus-Archiv Berlin / © Galerie Kicken, Berlin

Ludwig Mies van der Rohe, um 1930
Foto: Unbekannt / Stiftung Bauhaus Dessau

Lucia Moholy, Selbstportrait 1930
Bauhaus-Archiv Berlin / © VG BILD-KUNST, Bonn 2007

László Moholy-Nagy, ca. 1927
Foto: Lucia Moholy / © VG BILD-KUNST, Bonn 2007

Georg Muche, um 1926
Foto: Lucia Moholy / Bauhaus-Archiv Berlin / © VG BILD-KUNST, Bonn 2007

Richard Paulick, um 1931
Foto: Unbekannt / Gabriele Paulick, Berlin

Walter Peterhans, 1927
Foto: Grete Stern / Bauhaus-Archiv Berlin

Lilly Reich, um 1931
Foto: Ernst Louis Beck / Bauhaus-Archiv Berlin

Grete Reichardt, 1950er Jahre
Foto: Unbekannt / Stiftung Bauhaus Dessau

Xanti Schawinski, um 1924
Foto: Unbekannt

Hinnerk Scheper, 1927
Foto: Lucia Moholy / Bauhaus-Archiv Berlin / Dirk Scheper / © VG BILD-KUNST, Bonn 2007

Oskar Schlemmer, späte 1920er Jahre
Foto: Lily Hildebrandt / Bauhaus-Archiv Berlin

Joost Schmidt, um 1930
Foto: Grete Reichardt / Bauhaus-Archiv Berlin

Gunta Sharon-Stölzl, März 1930
Foto: Unbekannt

Wilhelm Wagenfeld, frühe 1920er Jahre
Foto: Unbekannt

Selected Literature Literaturauswahl

Baumann, Kirsten/Stiftung Bauhaus Dessau (Hg.): die bauhausbauten in dessau. Dessau 2002

Bittner, Regina/Stiftung Bauhaus Dessau (Hg.): Bauhausstil. Zwischen International Style und Lifestyle. Edition Bauhaus Band 11. Berlin 2003

Droste, Magdalena/Bauhaus-Archiv Berlin (Hg.): Bauhaus 1919–1933. Köln 1998

Engelmann, Christine/Schädlich, Christian: Die Bauhausbauten in Dessau. Berlin 1998

Fiedler, Jeannine und Peter Feierabend (Hg.): Bauhaus. Köln 1999

Gropius, Walter: Bauhausbauten Dessau. Bauhausbücher 12. Fulda 1930, Reprint Mainz 1997

Hahn, Peter/Bauhaus-Archiv Berlin (Hg.): bauhaus berlin. Auflösung Dessau 1932, Schließung Berlin 1933, Bauhäusler und Drittes Reich. Weingarten 1985

Isaacs, R. R.: Walter Gropius, Der Mensch und sein Werk. Berlin 1983, Band 1 und 2

Lietz, Bettina und Markgraf, Monika/ Stiftung Bauhaus Dessau (Hg.): Architekturoberflächen. Bauhausbauten Dessau – Fußböden. Dessau 2004

Markgraf, Monika und Schwarting, Andreas/Stiftung Bauhaus Dessau (Hg.): Bauforschungsarchiv Stiftung Bauhaus Dessau. Dessau 2002

Markgraf, Monika/Stiftung Bauhaus Dessau (Hg.): Archäologie der Moderne. Sanierung Bauhaus Dessau. Edition Bauhaus Band 23. Berlin 2006

Nerdinger, Winfried: Der Architekt Walter Gropius. 2. Aufl., Berlin 1996

Neumann, Eckhard (Hg.): Bauhaus und Bauhäusler. Köln 1985

Prigge, Walter/Stiftung Bauhaus Dessau (Hg.): Ikone der Moderne. Das Bauhausgebäude in Dessau. Edition Bauhaus Band 24. Berlin 2006

Rehm, Robin: Das Bauhausgebäude in Dessau. Die ästhetischen Kategorien Zweck Form Inhalt. Berlin 2005

Schöbe, Lutz/Thöner, Wolfgang (Hg.): Stiftung Bauhaus Dessau. Die Sammlung. Ostfildern 1995

Schwarting, Andreas/Stiftung Bauhaus Dessau (Hg.): Die Siedlung Dessau-Törten. Walter Gropius 1926-1928. Dessau 2001

Siebenbrodt, Michael (Hg.): bauhaus weimar. Entwürfe für die Zukunft. Ostfildern-Ruit 2000

Stiftung Bauhaus Dessau (Hg.): … das Bauhaus zerstört 1945 1947 das Bauhaus stört … Der Versuch einer Neueröffnung des Bauhauses in Dessau nach dem Ende des Zweiten Weltkrieges. Dessau 1996

Stiftung Bauhaus Dessau (Hg.): Umgang mit Bauten der Klassischen Moderne. Kolloquium am Bauhaus Dessau. Dessau 1999

Stiftung Bauhaus Dessau (Hg.): Bauhaus Objekte. Eine Auswahl aus der Sammlung der Stiftung Bauhaus Dessau auf CD. Berlin 2004

Stiftung Bauhaus Dessau/Kentgens-Craig, Margret (Hg.): Das Bauhausgebäude in Dessau 1926–1999. Basel/Berlin/Boston 1998

Thöner, Wolfgang: Das Bauhaus wohnt. Leben und Arbeiten in der Meisterhaussiedlung Dessau. Leipzig 2002

Wick, Rainer K.: Bauhaus Pädagogik. Köln 1994

Wingler, Hans Maria: Das Bauhaus. Weimar – Dessau – Berlin 1919–1933 und die Nachfolge in Chicago seit 1937. Köln 2002

Selected Literature in English Language

Bauhaus Dessau Foundation/Kentgens-Craig, Margret (Eds.): The Bauhaus Building in Dessau 1926–1999. Basel/Berlin/Boston 1998

Baumann, Kirsten/Bauhaus Dessau Foundation (Eds.): the bauhaus buildings in dessau. Dessau 2002

Droste, Magdalena/Bauhaus-Archiv Berlin (Eds.): Bauhaus. Cologne 1998

Fiedler, Jeannine and Peter Feierabend (Eds.): Bauhaus. Cologne 1999

Markgraf, Monika/Bauhaus Dessau Foundation (Eds.): Archaeology of Modernism. Renovation Bauhaus Dessau. Edition Bauhaus vol. 23. Berlin 2006

Neumann, Eckhard (Ed.): Bauhaus and Bauhaus People. Cologne 1992

Prigge, Walter/ Bauhaus Dessau Foundation (Eds.): Icon of Modernism. The Bauhaus Building Dessau. Edition Bauhaus vol. 24. Berlin 2006

Sharp, Dennis: Bauhaus, Dessau. Dessau 1925–1926, Walter Gropius (Architecture in Detail). Berlin 2002

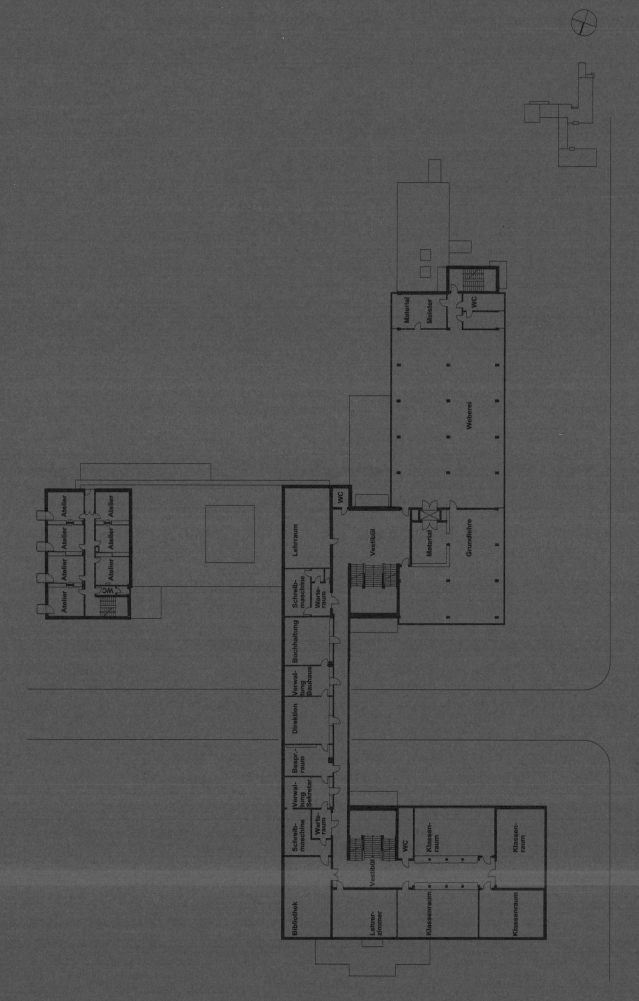

Atelier Atelier Atelier

Atelier Atelier Atelier

Atelier Atelier

WC

Material
Meister

WC

Weberei

Material

Grundlehre

Lehrraum

WC

Vestibül

Schreib-
maschine

Warte-
raum

Buchhaltung

Verwal-
tung
Bauhaus

Direktion

Bespr.-
raum

Verwal-
tung
Sekretär

Warte-
raum

Schreib-
maschine

Bibliothek

Lehrer-
zimmer

Vestibül

WC

Klassen-
raum

Klassen-
raum

Klassenraum

Klassenraum

Grundriss 1. Obergeschoss ▪ Ground Plan First Floor, 1926